MANNERS
FOR MEN

BY MRS. HUMPHRY
("MADGE" OF "TRUTH")

AUTHOR OF
"MANNERS FOR WOMEN"

Webb&Bower
EXETER, ENGLAND

Published in Great Britain 1979 by
Webb & Bower (Publishers) Limited,
33 Southernhay East, Exeter, Devon EX1 1NS

Distributed by WHS Distributors
(a division of W. H. Smith and Son Limited)
Euston Street, Freeman's Common, Aylestone Road,
Leicester LE2 7SS

Designed by Vic Giolitto

MANNERS FOR MEN first published 1897

This edition with additional material © Webb & Bower
(Publishers) Limited/Michael Levien 1979

ISBN 0 906671 00 0

Printed and bound in Great Britain by
Butler and Tanner Limited, Frome, Somerset

FOREWORD TO THE FACSIMILE EDITION

On its first publication *Manners for Men* enjoyed great success and was widely praised. Its author, Mrs Humphry, a well-known authority on etiquette, makes no bones about the qualities which constitute her ideal of manhood, the "gentleman". Gentleness and moral strength should be his salient characteristics, but they must be combined with "that polish that is never acquired but in one way: constant association with those so happily placed that they have enjoyed the influences of education and refinement all through their lives". Her aim was to help the less favoured to emulate her ideal. "There are thousands of young men in London alone," she writes, "who are longing to acquire the ease and *aplomb* of good society." Today Mrs Humphry's quiet rules of conduct may seem largely anachronistic. After all, most men are no longer concerned with the correct pronunciation of "brougham", nor with the once stylish practice of dropping the "g" at the end of present participles of verbs. Yet good behaviour was not confined to trivia – to the technique, say, of dissecting an orange or peeling a banana in the genteel fashion. It was primarily a matter of thoughtfulness and attentiveness and restraint, achieved with the aid of a rigorous code. There was a proper way for a man to behave on an omnibus, on horseback, on the river and in the street. The starting-point, however, was unequivocally his own home. *Manners for Men* is not only instructive and immensely entertaining, but affords astute and often humorous insights into another age.

MICHAEL LEVIEN   *Totnes, Devon 1979*

CONTENTS

MANNERS FOR MEN.

WOMAN'S IDEAL MAN.

I SUPPOSE there was never yet a woman who had not somewhere set up on a pedestal in her brain an ideal of manhood. He is by no means immutable, this paragon. On the contrary, he changes very often. **The ideal changes with the idealist.** If, however, the woman whose ideal he is grows upward in every way as she grows older, then these changes all go to improve him, and by the time he is finished he is a very fine creature. He never is finished till the brain of his creator ceases to work, till she has added her last touch to him, and has laid down the burden of life and gone elsewhere, perhaps to some happy land where ideals are more frequently realised than ever happens here.

Like every other woman, I have my ideal of manhood. The difficulty is to describe it. First of all, he **My ideal man.** must be a gentleman; but that means so much that it, in its turn, requires explanation.

Gentleness and moral strength combined must be the salient characteristics of the "gentleman," together with that polish that is never acquired but in one way : constant association with those so happily placed that they have enjoyed the influences of education and refinement all through their lives. He must be thoughtful for others, kind to women and children and all helpless things, tender-hearted to the old and the poor and the unhappy, but never foolishly weak in giving where gifts do harm instead of good—his brain must be as fine as his heart, in fact. There are few such men ; but they do exist. I know one or two. Reliable as rocks, judicious in every action, dependable in trifles as well as the large affairs of life, full of mercy and kindness to others, affectionate and well-loved in their homes, their lives are pure and kindly.

A man's brain should be as fine as his heart.

It was once said by a clever man that no one could be a gentleman all round who had not knocked about the world and associated with all sorts and conditions of men, high and low, rich and poor, good and bad. Experiences like these are like the processes for refining gold. The man who emerges unharmed from the fire of poverty and its associations, and who retains his independent manliness

The furnace of experience.

in relations with those high-placed, must have within him a fibre of strength that is the true essence of manliness. So many, alas! go down, down, when "puirtith cauld" touches them with her terrible, chilly finger. And so many become obsequious and subservient, false to themselves, in dealings with those above them.

Well! my ideal does neither. He is always true to himself, and "cannot then be false to any man." And he must have a sense of humour, too, otherwise he would be far **Humour an essential.** from perfect. How life is brightened by a sense of fun! Think of what breakfast, lunch, and dinner would be if life were to be as solemn and as serious as some folk would have it!

If good manners are not practised at home, but are allowed to lie by until occasion calls upon their wearer to assume them, they are **On behaviour in one's own home.** sure to be a bad fit when donned. It may be a trifle of the smallest to acquire a habit of saying "if you please" and "thank you" readily, but it is no trifling defect in a young man to fail to do so. If he does not jump up to open the door for his mother or sister, he may omit to do so some day when the neglect will tell against him in the estimation of those to please whom he would gladly give much. Carelessness in dress and personal appearance amount to bad manners. In the home there is sometimes a disagreeable negligence in this respect. At the breakfast-table unkempt hair, untended finger-nails, and a far from immaculate collar are occasionally to be seen, especially on late-comers who do not practise the ingratiating politeness of punctuality. Lounging, untidy habits are another form of bad manners. The ill-bred young man smokes all over the house, upstairs and downstairs, and even in his mother's drawing-room.

The ill-bred young man at home.

He may be traced from room to room by the litter of newspapers and magazines he leaves behind him. The present fashion of taking one's reading in pills, so to speak, snatching it in scrappy paragraphs from weekly miscellanies, is but too favourable to this lack of order. In this young man's own room there is chaos. The maids have endless trouble in clearing up after him. His tobacco is spilled over tables, chairs, and carpets. His handkerchiefs, ties, socks, and collars are lying about in every corner of the room. He is too indolent even to put his boots outside the door at night that they may be cleaned in the morning. To save himself trouble he bangs all the doors instead of gently latching them. And yet, perhaps, if he could but realise that all this is "bad manners," he would become as neat as he is now the reverse, and would be as decorative

at table as he is, at the present moment,
unornamental.

It is not only young men whose
standard of behaviour in the home
is a low one. Masters of the
house, fathers of families,
men of middle age, who are
terribly put out if any one
fails in duty to them, are sometimes
conspicuously ill-bred in everyday
matters. They are late for every meal,
to the discomfort of the other members
of the family and the great inconvenience of the servants. Polite to the
world outside, they are brusque and
disagreeable in their manner at home :
rough to the servants, rude to their
wives, and irritable with their children.
Sometimes a good heart and considerable family affection are hidden away
behind all this, but the families of such
men would be very glad to compound
for a little less affection and hidden
goodness and rather more gentleness
and outward polish.

"Young" men not alone culpable.

Apart from faults of temper, men
fall into careless habits of speech and
manner at home, and one form of
this, viz., habitually using strong
language in the presence
of women and children, is
particularly offensive. Be-
sides, it defeats itself ; for if the forcible
expressions are intended to express
disapprobation, they soon become
weak and powerless to do so, because
they are used on every possible occa-

On strong language.

5

sion. After a time they lose all meaning.

I know a family where there are sons and daughters, the latter charming and in every respect young gentlewomen. But the sons fall far below their level. They come to the door with thundering knocks that make every one in the house start disagreeably with surprise, walk through the hall without introducing their muddy boots to either scraper or doormat, sit down to meals without the usual preliminary of handwashing and hair-brushing, and are altogether rough and unpresentable. If friends call at the house these young men rush away from the chance of encountering them ; or, if they cannot help meeting them, they blush scarlet, look very *gauche* and uncomfortable, and feel miserable. They knock things over out of pure awkwardness, and never realise that the secret of the whole matter is the want of self-training. Girls are animated by a greater wish to please, an amiable desire that need not be confounded with vanity, and this wish has led the sisters of these young men to practise those small acts of daily self-denial which after awhile produce the highest self-culture so far as manners go. What is habitual neatness but constant coercion of human nature's innate indolence ? What is polite-

A typical family.

The secret of the whole matter.

The feminine motive.

ness in the home but the outcome of affection and self-respect, and the suppression of all those natural instincts of self-seeking that, allowed their way, produce the worst manners in the world ?

If any young man desires to be a perfect gentleman, he must begin in his own home. It is delightful to see some young men unobtrusively attentive to their sisters, watchful of every need of their father and mother, cheerful and pleasant in their manner, full of fun and brightness, yet never losing the gentleness that denotes the fine nature, and so beloved in the home for all these endearing qualities, that when they leave it they are sadly missed. The father misses them for the pleasant companionship ; the sisters miss them for the boyish spirits and the exuberant fun that never exceed the bounds of good taste and refinement ; and the mother misses them more than any one else, for no one better than she knows how many times a day her boys have set aside their own wishes in deference to hers, quietly, silently, unostentatiously —in a word, out of pure good manners, in the deepest, highest, truest sense of the words. Such gentle, virile natures look out at the world through the countenance, which is a letter of recommendation to them wherever they go.

The young man every one loves.

"Gentle, yet virile."

I have but faintly sketched my ideal.

The following pages may fill in the remaining touches.

Many men who go out into the world while still very young to earn their living have few opportunities of acquiring a knowledge of social observances.

Difficulties in the way.

Leaving home when boys, at an age when they are utterly careless of such things as etiquette and the "nice conduct of a cane," they live in lodgings or at boarding-houses of the cheaper sort, where the amenities of existence have to yield to its practicalities. Meals are served in a fashion that means despatch rather than elegance, economy rather than taste, and very few hints can be picked up for the guidance of young fellows when they enter the homes of friends and acquaintances. Their anxiety to fall in accurately and easily with the observances of those they meet on such occasions is as great as it is natural. They know well that to fail in these trifling acts of omission and commission is tacitly to acknowledge that they are unversed in the ways of good society. There is not necessarily any snobbishness in this. A man may be perfectly manly and yet most unwilling to show himself inferior in any way to others of the class to which he belongs by birth and education. Even should

"Where amenities yield to practicalities."

The penalty of ignorance.

The aspirant is not necessarily a snob.

8

those with whom he occasionally associates be his superiors, is he not right to try to rise ? Culture may mean little or nothing to the un- cultured. Polish may be an empty word to the un- polished. But they are realities, and go far to produce an inward and corresponding refinement of mind and spirit.

Culture and polish are realities.

There are thousands of young men in London alone at this very moment who are longing to acquire the ease and *aplomb* of good society. The desire is worthy of all encouragement. Only those with real good in them can feel it. The men who are destitute of it are those who associate with their inferiors, contentedly accept a low moral standard, adopt a mode of speech and action that is coarse and rough, and finally let themselves down to the frequenting of public-houses and places of amusement, where the entertainment has been carefully planned to suit the uneducated, the low-born, and others whose vitiated taste leads them to dislike what is lovely and of good report, and to revel in the reverse.

The desire to rise deserves encourage- ment.

But, unfortunately, many a good fellow has been driven to seek com- panionship with those be- neath him by the very diffi- culty he experiences in getting on in society. He fancies that his small solecisms are the subject of

Men to be pitied.

9

observation and comment, and he suffers agonies of *mauvaise honte*. Girls often laugh very unkindly at shy youths, when they might find opportunities of acting the good angel to them, and by the exercise of tact screening from observation those failures in good manners which are inevitable to the inexperienced. When he finds himself the butt of a few giggling girls, a young man feels miserably uncomfortable and humiliated, and he vows to himself that he will never again put himself in the way of such annoyance. Consequently he cuts good society, not realising that he would very soon overcome these initial difficulties and feel at home in it.

A word to girls.

He must find amusement somewhere. It is only natural to youth to crave it. At first his taste is jarred by those inferior to him, and his fastidiousness offended by their manners. But, such is the fatal adaptability of human nature to what is bad for it, he soon becomes accustomed to all that he at first objected to, and even forgets that he had ever found anything disagreeable in it. After a few months his speech begins to assimilate the errors of those about him in his leisure hours. He uses the very expressions that jarred upon him at first. His dress and carriage deteriorate, and he is well on his way

"We first endure, then pity, then embrace."

downhill in life long before he realises that he has quitted his own level, probably for ever.

And if only he had held his own at a few gatherings, and acquired experience, even at the cost **"If he had only held his own!"** of a little present pain and mortification, he would in the same interval of time be enjoying society, educating himself in its customs, and acquiring that exterior polish which comes of intimate acquaintance with its rules and ease in practising them.

Should this little manual of manners be of use to any such in enabling them **The object of this book.** to master the theory, as it were, of social customs in the educated classes, it will have attained its aim. I have always felt the greatest compassion for young men when first introduced, after school and college life, to the routine of dinner, dance, and ball. I have not forgotten the days when **Those early days!** shyness made my own heart sink at the prospect of a dinner-party and when the hardest task on earth was the finding of nothings to say to a partner at a ball. It is a miserable feeling of confusion and *gaucherie*, and if I can in any way avert it from others it will be a source of great gratification to me.

IN THE STREET.

THE rule of the road is a simple one, though it is often forgotten or neglected—"Keep to the right." **"The rule of the road."** Easy enough for women, it is complicated in the case of men by the necessity of always remaining on the kerb side of any lady they may be accompanying. Should the lady keep to the right in meeting or in passing other persons, her escort may either keep by her or go out in the road. He will be able to judge for himself which course will be advisable. His first duty is always **A man's duty is always to his lady.** to his companion, but that need not make him wanting in courtesy to other women. If remaining by the side of his companion should involve any inconvenience to the ladies of the other party, then he must give up his position, and go out into the roadway to let the latter pass. Should these be men, no consideration is necessary. He keeps close by his lady's side. In crowded **"In crowded streets."** streets he may often have to fall behind, but he should never allow any one to interpose

12

between her and him. Should the pressure from the crowd become extreme, his duty is to protect her from it as much as possible, but never by putting his arm round her waist. A hand on either side the lady's shoulders is usually sufficient.

In meeting acquaintances a nod is sufficient for a male friend, unless **Salutations.** his age or position is such as to render it advisable to raise the hat. Should a lady be with the acquaintance, any man meeting them must raise his hat. So must the individual walking with the lady. The etiquette of bowing is a simple one. Male acquaintances always wait for **The right of acknowledg-ment rests with the lady.** acknowledgment on the part of female, as well as from those men who are their superiors in age or position. But this does not mean that they are shyly to look away from them and to ignore them. On the contrary, they must show clearly by their manner that they are on the look-out for some sign of recognition and are ready **On waiting for acknow-ledgment.** to reply to it. Shyness often interferes with this and makes a young man look away, and this is occasionally misconstrued as indifference and resented as such. The calm, quiet, collected expression of face that suits the occasion is not achieved at once. Sometimes the over-anxiety to make a good impression defeats itself, producing a blushing eagerness better suited to a girlish than a manly countenance. This, however, is a youthful fault that is not without its ingratiating side, though young men view it in themselves and in each other with unbounded scorn. This sentiment of self-contempt is a frequent one in young people of both sexes. Their valuation of themselves varies as much as the barometer, and is as much affected by outward causes. After a "snub," real or fancied, it goes down to zero, but as a rule it speedily recovers itself, and in most young men enjoys an agreeable thermometer of 85° or so in the shade!

On self-contempt.

The well-mannered man never puts out his hand in greeting until a lady extends hers. This is a test of good breeding that is constantly applied. To those uninitiated in the ways of society, it would naturally appear the right thing to give as cordial a greeting as possible. Therefore the hand is held out, even on introduction to a perfect stranger. This is wrong. The first move in the direction of cordiality must come from the lady, the whole code of behaviour being based on the assumption that she is the social superior. The same holds good with elders and men of higher rank. When a man is introduced to these he raises his hat and bows, though slightly. It is only to kings and princes that a low bow is

Offering the hand.

made, or to those whose character and eminent position render an introduction to them a very high honour.

In introducing two men to each other the name of the inferior is mentioned first. By the inferior I mean the younger,

Introducing men to men.

the less important, or of lower rank. Suppose one of the two to be a familiar friend, and another a comparatively new acquaintance, then formality requires that the familiar friend shall be introduced to the other, being named first. The reason for this is that one naturally stands more on ceremony with the man one knows least. There may be counteracting circumstances, however, which would tend to reverse this order of things, but as a general rule, the social rank of both being equal, the above holds good.

Never introduce a lady to a gentleman; but always the gentleman to the lady. That is, mention the man's name first, addressing

Introducing men to ladies.

yourself to the woman— thus: "Allow me to introduce my friend Mr. Smith, Miss Jones." And follow this up immediately by saying, "Miss Jones," addressing Mr. Smith as you do so. It is a grave solecism to begin by introducing the lady. Tyros very naturally conclude that the lady's name should be first mentioned; but on thinking it over they will soon perceive that to do so would infer that she is the lesser consideration of the two.

It must always be borne in mind that the assumption of woman's social superiority lies at the root of these rules of conduct.

"Woman's social superiority."

It is bad manners to introduce people without permission. Nor must this permission be asked in the hearing of the second party. If Mr. A. wishes to know Miss B., the lady's leave must be obtained before he can be presented to her. The only exception to this rule is at a dance or ball, where introductions need not be regarded as leading to acquaintanceship. They are only for the dance, and may be ignored next day.

On permission to introduce.

Here, again, it is the lady's privilege to ignore her partner, if she choose. But if she should bow to him he must raise his hat, whether he desires to follow up the acquaintanceship or not. Objections more frequently arise on the woman's side; but should a man prefer to drop the matter he can manage to convey in his manner a disinclination to do so, and yet behave with perfect politeness. A man I knew was once introduced at a ball to a girl, with whom he danced two or three times. Before he met her again he heard that she had been actively concerned in circulating a slander about another girl whom circumstances had misrepresented. I

On recognition after a dance.

16

happened to see the next meeting between the two. The girl
Engineering an awkward point. bowed, smiled, and showed
some sign of an intention
to stop and talk. The
man raised his hat, looked extremely
solemn and unsociable, and passed on.
It was enough. The girl understood
that he did not wish to resume the
ball-room acquaintanceship, and very
probably guessed why. He did it
beautifully.

Before leaving the subject of the
promenade, I must clearly explain that
the hat must be raised even
The hat and the promenade. in saluting a very familiar
friend, if (*a*) that friend is ac-
companied by a lady, and (*b*)
when one is oneself accompanied by
a lady, even if she be only a mother
or sister. It is one of the signs of
caste that a man is equally polite to
his relatives as he is to the relatives of
others. We all know what
One's duty to one's own relatives. to think of a man who
omits small social duties
where his wife is concerned.
Even when he proves by paying them
duly to other women that he is aware
of what he ought to do, he is at once
set down as ill-bred—a "cad," in fact.
I once saw a Lord Mayor of London
enter his carriage before his wife, who
scrambled in after him as
A case in point. though well accustomed to
do so. One does not expect
the refinement of good manners from

civic dignitaries, as a rule, but this little action told the spectators more about the man than they would ever have found out in the newspapers. They at once perceived that he was unversed in the ways of good society.

But some one may suggest that this may have been on some state occasion, when his mayoral dignity obliged him to precede his wife. No. It was after a wedding. And besides, can any one fancy the Prince of Wales in any circumstances entering his carriage without having previously handed in the Princess, should she be his companion?

The lady first under every circumstance.

If accompanied by a dog, or dogs, their owner must hold himself responsible for their good behaviour. If his pets trespass in any way he must apologise for them, and do his best to repair any damage they have done. Should one of his dogs jump on a lady and make her gown muddy, he must offer his services and endeavour to get rid of the traces of the accident, if the lady wishes. Should she show a disinclination to accept his aid, he must at once withdraw, raising his hat as he does so. Should his dog attack another dog he must immediately call him off, administer correction, and apologise to the owner of the dog assaulted. I saw a young man once, in these circum-

When accompanied by dogs.

stances, beat the other dog, after his
own had jumped on it and bitten its
ear! He was dressed like a gentleman,
but his behaviour gave a truer indication
of him than did his garments.

Whistling and singing are incom-
patible with the conduct of a gentleman in the street, though
On whistling and singing. this by no means applies to
a quiet country road, where
ceremonious bearing is not required.
Nor is it permitted to wear the hands
in the pockets when walking
Carriage of the hands. in the Park, or the streets
of a town or city. This is
probably one of the reasons that the
cane or stick is still carried, though the
original cause, that of self-defence in
an age that was destitute of law and
order, fortunately exists no longer.
There are men who would not know
what to do with their hands if they had
not a cane or umbrella. This is partly
the fault of those who have charge of
boys when they are grow-
A word to parents. ing, and who allow them to
lounge about in slovenly
attitudes with their hands for ever in
their pockets. Then when they begin
to enter society they are quite at a
loss. At schools where
And school-masters. boys are regularly drilled
the whole effect of the
drilling is done away with by the way
in which the boys are allowed to
sit and stand in the most remarkable
attitudes of slouching awkwardness.

It is only when they are at drill or out walking with the masters that any notice is taken of their carriage. And yet it is an important point with regard to health that the shoulders should be held well back, the chest forward, and the head up.

Should a man be so fortunate as to be of some service to **On rendering slight services.** any lady in the street, such as picking up a parcel or sunshade she may have dropped, or helping her out of any small difficulty, he must raise his hat and withdraw at once. Such trifling acts as these do not by any means constitute an acquaintanceship, and to remain by her side when the incident is over would look like presuming on what he had done, as though it gave him a right to her continued acknowledgments. This would be ungentlemanly.

At the same time, these occurrences are sometimes deliberately planned by girls and women with a direct view to scraping acquaintance with young men. It is scarcely necessary to say that girls who stoop to this kind of **On girls making advances.** manœuvring are hardly ever gentlewomen. Members of good families have been known to do such things in the wild exuberance of youth and high spirits, but they cannot hope to retain the respect of those who know them when they deliberately lower themselves in such ways as these. Picking up pro miscuous male acquaintances

The risk to one's good name. is a practice fraught with danger. It cannot be denied that girls of the lower middle classes are often prone to it; and there are thousands of young men who have no feminine belongings in the great towns and cities where they live, and who are found responsive to this indiscriminating mode of making acquaintances. But

The method can produce little good they must often hesitate before choosing as wife a girl who shows so little discretion as to walk and talk with young men of whom she knows nothing beyond what they choose to tell her.

The seaside season is prolific in these chance acquaintanceships—

Seaside "Flirtations." "flirtations," as they may perhaps be called. Bicycling is well known to favour them. But as they are far removed from the practices of the class of society to which belong those gentlemen of whom this little book treats, they may be dismissed with a few words of advice. Should any young man become acquainted with a girl in this manner, let him show his innate chivalry by treating her in every way as he would wish his own sister to be

Should the man become attached. treated in similar circumstances. If he becomes attached to her, let him first find out all about her that he possibly

21

can, and should what he hears be en-
couraging, then let him ask her to introduce him to her family as a suitor for her
hand. Should the girl fall in love with
him, let him protect her against herself
like a *preux chevalier*, like an honourable and high-minded English gentleman. If he feels that he cannot reciprocate her sentiment, he
should give up seeing her.
Should she, as some girls
of the kind have been known
to do, pursue him with letters making
appointments, she makes his task of
renunciation a difficult one, but he
should fulfil it nevertheless.

Should he be unable to reciprocate.

It is difficult in this way. Suppose
a girl writes to a young man : " Meet
me at the tea-rooms, No. 440, Bond
Street, to-morrow afternoon." There
is no chance of replying in time to prevent her going there, and to
absent himself would be to
administer a severe snub
to a girl whom he likes very well, and
who has flattered his self-love in many
ways during their acquaintanceship.
What can he do ? It is a point that he
must decide for himself, taking all the
circumstances into consideration, and
not forgetting to regard her ultimate
welfare in the matter at least as much
as his own actual wishes.

"Her ultimate welfare."

This may seem to some young men
a very " high-falutin' " view to take of
such a small matter as meeting a young
woman and having tea together. Most

of them, finding that a girl was grow-
ing fond of them, would
The view of the ordinary young man. encourage the feeling by
every means in their power,
regardless of whether it
could ever end in marriage, and careless of everything beyond the gratification of their own vanity. But there
are bright exceptions to these who do
not allow themselves to be carried
away by the flattery implied in a girl's
attentions, and who can consider her
welfare in selfless fashion. Sometimes
fastidious taste comes to
The manly young man does his own wooing. their aid and makes with-
drawal from an interesting
companionship compara-
tively easy. For, after all, the manly
young man has a prejudice in favour
of doing his own wooing !

It is not at all necessary that a man
should accept invitations from a girl to
meet her at restaurants, sub-
Invitations from girls. scription dances, bazaars, or
any other place. If a girl
so far forgets herself, and is so lacking
in modesty and propriety as to make
appointments with young men in such
ways as these, she cannot be worth
much, and may lead the young man
into a very serious scrape. A public
horse-whipping is an extremely disagreeable thing, and yet cases have
been known when such have been
administered by irate brothers or
fathers, when the only fault committed
by the young man had been to obey

the commands of a forward and bold young woman—one of the sort to whom Hamlet would have said, "Get thee to a nunnery."

Such invitations are better ignored, though it is difficult for the average young man to resist the temptation of being courted and flattered, and of seeking the society of girls who administer these pleasant attentions. But if their standard is a high one, they would say to themselves : "What should I like another fellow to do, supposing the girl were my sister?" (Almost always he mentally adds, "God forbid!") This clears up the question for him at once. If he is high-minded and honourable he keeps away. If he is unscrupulous and self-indulgent he meets the girl and lets the acquaintanceship drift on to dangerous ground.

They are better ignored.

Such girls as these can never tell if a man whose past and present and surrounding circumstances are unknown to her is a scoundrel or otherwise. Fortunately, the code of manners obtaining amongst the educated and well-brought-up forbids all such indiscriminate acquaintance-making. Girls who stoop to it are usually those who have failed to secure attention in their own circle, and are, as a rule, the sort of girl who marries a groom or

The danger of the proceeding.

The offenders.

24

runs away with a good-looking foot-man.

A young man once asked me if it would be etiquette to offer an unknown lady an umbrella in the street, supposing she stood in need of one. I replied : "No *lady* would accept the offer from a stranger, and the other sort of person might never return the umbrella." In large towns women of breeding soon learn to view casual attentions from well-dressed men with the deepest distrust. They would suffer any amount of inconvenience rather than accept a favour from a stranger, knowing that so many men make it their amusement to prowl about the streets, looking after pretty faces and graceful figures, and forcing their attentions on the owners. Contemptible curs they are, whether young or old, and they are of all ages. Very young girls have sometimes extremely unpleasant experiences with such men, not only in the streets but in omnibuses, trams, and trains. Cultivating a gentlemanly exterior, they can yet never be gentlemen, and a good, pure woman finds something hateful in the look of their eyes, the whole expression of their faces. It cannot be denied, however, that there is a corresponding class of women and girls who make promiscuous male acquaintances in the

Offering an unknown lady an umbrella.

A contemptible class of men.

Their female counterparts.

streets, and the young man learns to distinguish these from respectable members of the community almost as soon as the young girl learns to dread and fear the prowling man. The existence of such a state of things makes self-respecting women most careful to accept no advances from a stranger, and the true gentleman, understanding this, refrains from offers of assistance that he would gladly make were society so constituted as to be free from such pests as the above.

Offers of service from strangers not therefore allowable.

In passing ladies on the promenade, in the street or Park, if a man chance to be smoking, he always takes his cigar from his mouth, replacing it when the lady or ladies have passed on. In the crowded streets of great cities this, if carried out in full entirety, would be too much. Therefore it is observed only with reference to such ladies as pass the smoker quite closely. "I know he is a gentleman," said a girl once of a good-looking young fellow whose appearance had pleased her—"I know he is a gentleman, for he stopped smoking directly he saw us." It is in the observance of little things of this kind that one shows clearly one's breeding or lack of it.

On removing a cigar when passing a lady.

When a young man is walking with a lady, and happens to meet another lady with whom he is on more intimate terms than with his companion, he must ask pardon of the latter if he should stop to speak. "Excuse me for one moment," he would say, and his companion, if a gentlewoman, would walk some yards on, and then slowly stroll along until he joined her again. The strict rule is that when walking with a lady a man should never leave her side.

Meeting a more intimate acquaintance when with a lady.

Suppose a young man were to meet his mother or sister while he was in the company of a lady unknown to them, he must not introduce her to them or them to her without having previously obtained special permission on both sides. There are young men who make acquaintance with girls in a lower walk of life than their own. It would be an insult to mother or sister to introduce a milliner's apprentice or an assistant in a shop, or, in fact, any one whom he had picked up without a regular introduction. No respectable young woman would walk with or talk with any man to whom she had not had a proper introduction. The inference is that those who do so are not respectable, and must not, therefore, be introduced to those who are.

The rule for introductions in such a case.

Acquaintance without introduction.

The old rule was that when a gentleman stopped to speak to a lady in the street he walked a little way with her in the direction in which she

Stopping to speak to a lady.

had been going. But now this is less observed than it used to be. The lady herself, if she wishes the conversation to be a short one, stops at once, **The old rule and the new.** knowing that it will be easier for a man to terminate it in these circumstances than if he were sauntering by her side.

IN A CARRIAGE.

IN handing ladies to their carriage a man offers his right arm to the senior of the party and walks with **Handing ladies to their carriage.** her to the door, opening it with his left hand. The others will probably follow without escort, but if not, he must offer it to each in turn, holding an umbrella over them should it be raining. He closes the door and conveys their orders to the footman or coachman. Should he be invited to enter the carriage with them, he al- **The man takes the back seat.** ways takes the back seat— that is, with his back to the horses—unless specially invited to the front one. He must not either raise or lower the windows unless requested to do so. Should he be **On smoking in a carriage.** smoking, he throws away his cigar or cigarette at once. If he should be a very intimate acquaintance of the lady, he may ask her permission to smoke, but never otherwise, since it is disagreeable for a woman to refuse such permission, and consequently she often gives it when she really dislikes the smell of tobacco.

especially in the limited space of a carriage, should it be a closed one.

It may be as well to mention here that the proper pronunciation of the word "brougham" is as *Pronuncia-* though it were spelled *tion of* "broom," quite short and *"brougham."* monosyllabic. This is a trifle, of course, but, like many another equally small matter, it is indicative of those accustomed to good society.

IN A HANSOM.

IN handing a lady into a hansom care must be taken to protect her dress from the muddy wheel. The gentleman asks if she would like the glasses down, and conveys her instructions to the driver, then raises his hat as she drives away. Should he be accompanying her in the hansom, she seats herself at the nearest side to the pavement, so that when he enters he will not have to go round a corner, as it were. In this case he gives the cabman instructions across the roof of the cab, and if his companion wishes the glasses to be lowered, he asks for them through the trap-door at the top of the cab. He must never smoke when the glasses are let down— to do so would render the atmosphere unbearable to almost any woman. But if he knows his partner in the drive sufficiently well, he can ask permission to smoke, should the glasses not be required.

Guarding the lady's dress.

When accompanying the lady.

SMOKING.

THE etiquette in this, as in many other matters, has quite altered during the last few years. At one time *The domain of Princess Nicotine.* it was considered a sign of infamously bad taste to smoke in the presence of women in any circumstances. But it is now no longer so. So many women smoke themselves, that in some houses even the drawing-room is thrown open to Princess Nicotine. The example of the Prince of Wales has *The leader of the fashion.* been largely instrumental in sweeping away the old restrictions. He smokes almost incessantly. On one occasion, at the Ranelagh Club, I noticed that he consumed four cigars in rapid succession, almost without five minutes' interval between them. The only time that he left off smoking, during the three hours that he remained in the Pavilion with the Princess and other ladies, was for ten minutes when tea was handed round.

It is now no uncommon thing to see a man in evening dress smoking in a brougham with a lady on *The lengths to which a smoker may now go.* their way to opera, theatre, or dinner engagement. This is going rather far, for a woman's evening dress implies shut windows, except in the height of summer, and her garments become as much impregnated with the odour of tobacco as if she had herself been smoking.

Some men have a knack of ridding their clothes and themselves of the fumes of smoke in a wonderful way. Perhaps one reason of this is that the tobacco they use is of a mild sort. Perhaps the diligent use of the clothes-brush is another. But there are also men round whom cling the odours of stale tobacco with a very disagreeable constancy. Why it should be so I cannot pretend to say. It must be due to carelessness of some kind, and carelessness in such matters amounts to bad manners. Even to men who smoke—and much more to those who do not—the smell of stale tobacco is revolting. Fancy, then, how it must offend the olfactory nerves of women. Such men suggest the stableyard while they are yet several feet away !

On getting rid of the smell,

Try the clothes-brush.

A very delicate, even exquisite, personal cleanliness is characteristic of the true gentleman, and more particularly the English gentleman, who is noted all the world over for his devotion to his "tub" and his immaculate propriety in all matters of the toilette. This is not claiming too much for my countrymen.

Personal cleanliness a hall-mark of the English gentleman.

It is acknowledged by other nations that ours is superior in this respect. Once, indeed, I heard a curious inversion of this. At a foreign hotel one waiter said to the other in their mutual language : "What dirty fellows these English must be to want such a lot of washing ! I've carried up four cans of water to No. 47 this morning !"

Sauntering up the street of a small German town one day, two English ladies saw, a couple of hundred yards away, a party of men standing admiring an ancient gateway. "They must be English," said one of the ladies ; and before she could finish her sentence the other finished it for her in the very words she had been about to utter : "They are so beautifully clean !"

"They must be English."

This characteristic is carried to an extreme in the close clipping of the hair ; but as fashion ordains that it must be worn very short, its behests must be obeyed by all who wish to be in society and of it. "Who is that long-haired fellow?" is the question invariably asked about any man whose visits to the barber are infrequent. "Must be an artist or a music man," is the frequent commentary. Sometimes he is merely careless of conventionalities, and by being so proves that he is rather "out of it" where good society is concerned. The rule appears

The close-cropped head.

The "long-haired fellow."

34

to be that directly a man finds that he has any hair worth brushing, he must immediately go and have it cut. It would be much more becoming if allowed to grow a little longer, but things being as they are, only the few can afford to defy the ordinary custom.

THE humble omnibus may be thought by some readers too democratic a kind of conveyance to be *The humble omnibus.* considered in a book on Manners. Not at all ! There are several reasons why it should have a place in such a volume. The first is, that during the last ten years or so the omnibus has been largely *It is now used by all classes.* used by women of the educated, cultured, and well-dressed classes. Another and stronger reason is that no considerations of the kind should affect a man's manners. If he can behave like a gentleman in a carriage, he is almost certain to do so in an omnibus, and *vice versâ*. It is even more difficult in the humbler vehicle. In a carriage one *A fine field for true courtesy.* is seldom crowded up to the degree that often occurs in the plebeian " 'bus." In fact, there are far more opportunities for the display of good manners in the latter than in the former. Many of them are of a negative character. True courtesy, for instance, will prevent a man from infringing the rights of his neighbours on either side by occupying more than his

own allotted space. Very stout men
are obliged to do so, but at least they
need not spread out their
The man who knees in a way that is calcu-
wants all the
room. lated to aggravate the evil.
Nor need they arrange them-
selves in a comfortable oblique position,
with the result of enhancing the inconvenience they must necessarily cause to
those near them. Even a thin man can
take up a quantity of room by thus dis-
posing himself at an angle of forty-five
with the other occupants of an omnibus.

The morning paper may be converted
into an offensive weapon in the hands
of the rude and careless, who open it
out to its fullest width, re-
The "news- gardless of the comfort of
paper"
offender. those sitting next them.
Newspapers are rather un-
wieldy things to turn and twist about
in a limited space, but this very circumstance affords a man an opportunity of
displaying his skill in manipulating the
large, wide sheets, without dashing
them in the face of his nearest neighbour, or knocking up against anybody
in a series of awkward movements that
a little care could easily convert into
leisurely, graceful ones.

There is another way in which men
are apt to be careless, and that is in the
disposal of a wet umbrella.
The wet Women are even more so,
umbrella
nuisance. but these remarks are intended particularly for men,
and beyond acknowledging that mem-

bers of my own sex are equal sinners,
I must leave them out of the question.
When any one takes a dripping umbrella
into an omnibus, he must charge himself with the task of seeing that it
annoys no one but himself. If he can,
at the same time, protect himself, well
and good ; but he must be altruistic in
the matter and care for others first ;
the alternative being to prove himself
lacking in one form of good manners.
He must not even let his wet umbrella
lean up against a vacant part
of the cushioned seat, rendering it damp for the next
comer. His social conscience cannot
be up to its work if he permits himself
to ignore the right of the absent to
consideration, merely because they are
absent.

The rights of the absent.

Allowing umbrellas and sticks to
protrude so as to trip up unwary
passengers is another thing
to be avoided. Carrying a
stick or umbrella under the
arm with the ferule protrud-
ing at the back and threatening the
eyes of those who walk behind, is
always a reprehensible practice, and
one that is fraught with danger, and it
is perhaps more than ever dangerous
when the proprietor is ascending or
descending the steps of an omnibus.
At such moments passengers are liable
to sudden checks from various causes,
and the resultant backward jerk can be
quite annoying enough to those behind

Carrying umbrellas and sticks.

without the aggravation of a pointed stick assaulting them. I have seen a girl's hat torn off her head in this way, its numerous securing pins making havoc in her coiffure and eliciting lively expressions of pain.

It might appear hardly necessary to advocate care in walking up past other passengers inside an omnibus, for fear of treading on their feet, and to recommend a word of apology in case of any such transgression. But there have been cases which point to the desirability of a word of advice on such points.

Entering and leaving an omnibus.

The ready apology covers a multitude of social sins. From some men it comes with an expression of such earnest solicitude that, anxious to reassure them, one quite willingly makes light of the damage done.

Apology covers a multitude of social sins.

In escorting a lady a man hands her into the omnibus before entering it himself; and if she prefers the top, he lets her mount the staircase in front of him. There seems to be an idea in the lowly classes that it is correct to precede a lady in ascending steps or stairs. This is not in accordance with the practice of good society. If circumstances do not admit of the two walking abreast, then the lady goes first, both in ascending and descending any stairs.

The lady first, entering and leaving.

It is by no means necessary that any

man should resign his seat in or on an omnibus simply because a woman wishes for it. The con-

On giving up one's seat to a lady.

ductor has no right to ask "if any gentleman will go outside to oblige a lady"; and no gentlewoman would allow him to ask such a favour on her behalf. The inside passengers have selected inside seats, thereby testifying to their preference for them, and they should be allowed to retain them without interference. I have seen a delicate-looking boy, racked with a hacking

Women offenders.

cough, induced to ride outside on a cold and rainy night in order that a fat, rosy, healthy woman might have his inside seat. I felt all the more indignant on his behalf because the woman never even thanked him. It was no business of mine, but I was rejoiced to hear a man's voice mutter in the darkness, "She looks better able to face it than that pale-faced lad." But the woman wore a smug, well-pleased air, little knowing that her fellow-passengers were almost all regarding her with a feeling of dislike.

I repeat that no lady, in the highest sense of the term, would ever permit the conductor of an omnibus

No lady would request this favour.

to ask such a favour for her. She would not ask it for herself; unlike a woman whom I saw, one day, mount on the step of an omnibus and inquire of the "insides," "Won't any genelman ride outside to oblige a lydy?" the "lydy" being herself.

It can never be out of place for a man to give up his seat in favour of the old and infirm, or for a woman with a baby in her arms. But such matters as these belong to a region of heart and mind beyond mere manners, and it is useless to suggest any line of action on such subjects. The impulse must come from within.

Higher laws than etiquette.

There have been women so unreasonable as to complain of men smoking on the top of an omnibus. Could anything be more illogical? First, they invade the seats that have been claimed by man as his right (though perhaps unjustly) for many long years, and then they feel annoyed because he smokes in their presence. Or, to speak accurately, they are petulant because his tobacco is often rank, strong, and consequently evil-smelling. But no man need feel it necessary to put out his pipe or throw away his cigar in these circumstances. Should he find himself so placed that the wind blows his smoke in the face of a woman, he may propose to change seats with her, in order that she may be spared the inconvenience. But no woman could rationally expect him to do more.

Smoking on the top of an omnibus.

A man is justified in so doing.

ON HORSEBACK.

A GREAT change has taken place during the last few years in the character of riding costume for the Park.

Riding costume for the Park. The subject may scarcely be a suitable one for a little book intended for those unaccustomed to the usages of the society of the wealthy. But there are almost always exceptional cases in which such information may be found of use. Only quite old-fashioned people ride in black coats,

Disappearance of the black coat. the usual gear consisting of knickerbocker suits with Norfolk, or other country jacket, brown tops and bowler hats. It must be admitted that this is a distinct gain in picturesqueness. Straw hats are often seen on riders in the Park, but these have not quite so good an effect. The old formalities in dress are rapidly

The scope and limitations of the tweed suit. disappearing. A man may ride in town in a tweed suit, which once would have been considered highly heterodox. He may even walk about London in the height of the season in a tweed suit, but it is not considered correct for him to join his friends in the Park without reverting to the black coat and high hat. Many an old statesman is still to be seen in the Park riding in frock-coat and tall hat, just as John Leech depicted the men of his day.

There are certain rules of etiquette connected with riding on horseback, which no one can afford to ignore. It is extremely ill-mannered to gallop noisily past a mounted lady, the risk being of startling her horse and inconveniencing her, if not subjecting her to an accident. The rule of the road for equestrians is to keep to the left, exactly the opposite to that for pedestrians. In passing others in front a detour is made to the right ; in meeting other riders or wheel traffic of any sort the rider keeps close to the left. In accompanying a lady the gentleman keeps on her right hand, whether in town or on country roads.

The rule of the road for equestrians.

At a meet of hounds, where ladies in carriages often assemble, it is not polite to keep too near them if mounted on a fidgety horse. When the hounds throw off, the inexperienced in such matters has a disagreeable way of getting in front in his eagerness, and sometimes overriding the hounds. This, in the eyes of the huntsman, is not a fault ; it is a crime of the blackest dye. If commissioned to take charge of a lady in the hunting-field a man

At a meet of hounds.

"A crime of the blackest dye."

must sacrifice his sporting instincts to a certain extent in order to see her safe over her fences, giving her a lead, or following her lead as circumstances may dictate. His desire to be in at the death may be as great as hers, but he must not indulge it at the expense of his politeness. Very often his charge may beg of him to go on and leave her to her own devices. If he should perceive that she is really uncomfortable about keeping him back he may possibly yield to her persuasion, but in the case of any accident happening to her he would be certainly called to account by those who had placed her in his charge.

A man's duty to his charge.

His responsibility ends only with the hunt.

One of the mistakes made by novices in the hunting-field is that of getting themselves up in "pink," though they may not be a member of any hunt. This is more particularly the case when the packs are near town. Good West End tailors would never allow their clients to make such mistakes as these. They are the best authorities on all the minutiæ of country riding costume, and it is well for the customer to put himself unreservedly in the hands of the long-experienced in such matters. Of course this means high charges. Experience and skill are commercial commodities, just as much as fine cloth and silk linings,

A common error.

Advice to the novice.

44

but if a man can afford to go a-hunting he ought to be able to afford the advice of a good tailor.

In mounting a lady on horseback the gentleman takes her left foot in his right hand, and when she springs he helps her in this manner to reach the saddle, afterwards adjusting her left foot in the stirrup and arranging her habit for her.

Assisting a lady to her mount.

DRIVING.

THE same rule of the road applies to driving as to riding. In the crowded traffic of large towns and cities it would be difficult, if not impossible, to observe the good old rule of courtesy that prohibits the driver of any private carriage from overtaking and passing that of a friend or neighbour on the road. The members of the Four-in-Hand and Coaching Clubs still observe it, and seldom pass each other without an apologetic wave of the hand or raising of the hat. A gentleman driving a mail phaeton in the Park with a lady by his side must, of course, acknowledge all salutes by raising his hat, if he is sufficiently expert to admit of his doing so without risk. It is not every one who can emulate the Prince of Wales, who, when driving a coach, can take a cigar from his lips and raise his hat with the whip-hand, the reins, of course, being in the left. It is not unusual, nowadays, to see a man driven by a lady. In such a case he must be on the alert to afford her every assistance in his power. In handing

"Keep to your left."

Acknowledging salutes.

Handing a lady up to her coach seat.

46

a lady up to her place on a coach some expertness is required, especially where the usual short ladder is not available, and she has to mount first on the wheel and then on to the coach itself.

The box-seat of a coach to the left of the driver is considered the place of honour, and the lady invited to occupy it is very appreciative, as a rule, of this mark of attention. It is scarcely necessary to remark that a man must be as careful about the invitations for a drive on his four-in-hand as he would be in other circumstances. A lady would resent being asked to meet any one unsuitable in a drive, even though the latter may be relegated to a back seat. Sometimes ladies are very anxious to take the reins and drive themselves, a circumstance which has often occasioned agonies of nervousness to other women on the coach. It is quite possible to refuse such a request in a polite and gentlemanly way, partly by seeming to ignore it or laughing it off. It is not a bad plan when some such request is supposed to be imminent to bind oneself beforehand by a promise to one of the timid ladies. This promise can be produced with great effect when occasion arises. A man usually dismounts when calling for a lady to take her for a ride,

Invitations to coach drives.

A man may refuse a lady the coach reins.

On dismounting, when calling for a lady.

if she is to be mounted. Sometimes, however, this rule is remitted, as in the case of a restive and very fresh animal; the groom then assists the lady to mount. The driver of a four-in-hand very seldom dismounts in such circumstances, though, of course, there are exceptions to this as to almost all other rules.

It used to be considered bad manners to smoke when driving with a lady. This is now quite antedilu-

On smoking when driving. vian, so to speak. Permission must, of course, always be asked of the lady. It is scarcely ever refused, and it is almost an exceptional thing to see a man driving without a cigar between his teeth.

Should the lady driven meet some acquaintances unknown to her charioteer, and wish to stop and converse with them, he raises his hat and awaits her pleasure. She will probably introduce him, but if not he takes no part in the conversation. The only thing he can do is to remain passive, but unless the lady feels justified in introducing him it is an error of taste on her part to enter into conversation with her friends.

Some ladies have a great disinclination to mount a four-in-hand or mail phaeton until the driver is

In which case the rule may be broken. seated with the reins in his hand and in full command of the horses. There is nothing surprising in this, for, after all, the groom who stands at the head of

48

the horses before the start has very little control over them, and one or two disagreeable accidents have occurred in this way, the horses taking fright and escaping from his grasp. Consequently it would be no breach of good manners for the gentleman driving to take his seat and thus reassure his nervous companion.

A MAN who can play a good game
of chess, or even an excellent rubber

**Chess And
whist per-
manently
popular.**
of whist, must be aware
that the acquirement in-
volves an education in itself. Neither is ever likely
to become unpopular among the best
classes of society. Chess and whist
clubs increase in number as time goes
on ; but for the purposes of everyday
life less exigent games are found more
useful. Billiards, backgammon, poker,
bézique, baccarat, écarté, draughts,
vingt-et-un, and loo may be mentioned

**One should
be able to
play the
minor games.**
among the minor accom-
plishments with which the
modern young man finds it
convenient to be equipped.
That a bad use has been made of some
of these by converting them into media
for gambling is not to be denied. At
the same time there is no reason why
those who play them in moderation
should refrain from doing so because
others abuse rather than use these

**These things
are innocent
in them-
selves.**
means of recreation A
round game affords a very
innocent mode of spending
an enjoyable evening, and
country-house life especially is often

enlivened in this way. Home life, whether in town or country, is apt to become monotonous, particularly for the young members of the

And often quite necessary.

family, if there is not occasionally an amusing game got up to pass away the evening hours, and anything that adds to the attractions of home must at least have one excellent recommendation.

Apart from other considerations, the demeanour of a young man when playing cards affords a very

A man's breeding is shown in his play.

good test of his manners. Some of them appear to think that the only fun to be had out of the game lies in cheating —very open and transparent cheating, to be sure—but still sufficient to spoil the amusement of others. A curious development of money greed is sometimes observable in players, who will show extreme exasperation at the loss of so simple a coin as a penny. There are many fairly good-

Irritability over games.

tempered men (and women) who evince extreme irritability over games of any kind. To play with such as these is very disagreeable, and the tendency to irascibility should be firmly checked by those who wish to be popular in society.

The host or hostess always takes the lead in these games, or else deputes some one else to do so. It is a sign of ill-breeding when any outsider assumes the command of a game without having been asked to do so.

An outsider may not take the lead unsolicited.

Unfortunately, gambling games are very popular at some houses, and it is possible for a young man, being unaware of the fact, to be drawn in and lose more than he can afford before he can politely extricate himself. In such circumstances the only thing he can do is religiously to avoid any such house in future. It is a matter of notoriety that there are men who make good incomes by fleecing the young and inexperienced whom they invite to their houses under the guise of hospitality ; but even when there is no deliberate dishonesty in question, as in these cases, the host or hostess, out of pure love of gambling, draws in the guests to play for high sums. Unpardonable, it is true, but such things have to be reckoned with, and avoided, if possible. The matter is not confined to London ; country-house life has much to answer for under the same heading.

Men and houses to be avoided.

Things to be reckoned with.

RULE OF THE ROAD ON THE RIVER.

THERE is a rule of the road for the river, and those who boat on the Thames on crowded days fervently wish that it were better understood. There does not appear to be any means of acquiring the necessary information. If such means exist they have never come under my notice, and, for at least one summer, I spent many hours daily in that agreeable form of exercise. Boats coming down with the tide keep the middle of the river; those going against it hug the shore on either side, but in passing other boats coming in the same direction they must go out in a semicircle, leaving the front boat the shore. Tow-boats are always given this advantage. In meeting other boats coming down-stream which really have no right to the shore, but are mistakenly kept near the margin by inexperienced steerers, the boat going up-stream should not go out, but keep towards the land.

The rule of the road on the river.

With the tide—the middle of the stream.

Up-stream—either shore.

The rights of anglers.

53

The rights of the numerous anglers should be respected; and it is not only courteous but politic to do so, as it is disagreeable to have the lines entangled in the boat. Row-boats give

Sailing-boats.

way to sailing-boats on the river, especially when the latter are tacking to use the breeze. As to steam-launches, their motto too often appears to be that "Might is right." Occupants of small boats keep a sharp look-out for these.

In passing through the locks the usual politeness of refraining from

Passing through locks.

shooting ahead of boats in front should be observed. Any active emulation of this kind is a very risky

business in the same way when pulling a boat over the rollers. A man is bound to yield the *pas* to ladies or to any boat containing ladies. In fact, the courtesies of the river may be summed up as similar to those on land.

DINNER-PARTIES.

"MRS. X. requests the pleasure of Mr. L.'s company at dinner on Thursday, the 16th of February, at eight o'clock."

Invitation.

"Mr. L. accepts with pleasure Mrs. X.'s kind invitation to dinner on Thursday, the 16th of February."

Acceptance.

These are the preliminaries; the lady's address being on the sheet of paper or card on which her invitation has been written. Three weeks' notice is usual, but sometimes, in the season, when many parties are going on, invitations are sent out four, five, or six weeks beforehand, in order to secure the guests. In the case of "lions" even longer invitations have been given; but as one of the first principles of good breeding is never to "corner" anybody, it is scarcely fair to invite those who are in much request without giving them the option of refusal. An invitation of seven or

Address of the hostess.

The usual interval.

Unfairly long invitations.

eight weeks' length scarcely allows one
to plead a pre-engagement, and often
defeats the eager hostess's own end by
indrcing the "lion" to accept without
any intention of being present, writing
later on to "renage," to use a good old
whist term.

But as our young man is scarcely
yet a "lion," and probably not over-
burdened with engagements for dinner
or any other social function, we may
imagine him accepting with a free mind.
Should anything intervene to prevent
him carrying out his engagement, he
is in duty bound to let his
Breaking the engagement. hostess know as early as
possible that he cannot be
present at her dinner-party. This
is more especially and particularly
necessary with dinners, though it
holds good with regard to all invitations. But with dinner there is
a peculiar obligation laid
Peculiar obligation of the diner-out. upon the guests. The
choice and arrangement of
them involves care on the
part of the dinner-giver, more so
than in the case of any other meal.
In fact, dinner stands alone as an
institution sacred to the highest rites
of hospitality. To be invited is an
honour to the young man who is
just beginning his social life. To
absent himself would be a gross
rudeness, unless he could plead circumstances of a pressing nature. It
is considered a great infraction of

good manners to wire on the very day of the party that one

On declining at the last moment. cannot dine as arranged, unless something has occurred to justify such conduct. The hostess can with difficulty find a substitute at short notice, and the whole plan of her table is destroyed by the absence of one person. There are few people who would not feel offended at being invited to fill a gap of the kind, and this is what makes it so extremely discourteous to disappoint at the last moment, as it were. The unfortunate hostess thinks, " Is there any one good-natured enough to come and fill the vacant place ? " Sometimes this is the *raison d'être* of a young man's first invitation. Let him accept

A " fill-up " invitation. it by all means, even though he is perfectly aware that he was not his entertainer's first choice.

Many a young man feels nervous about his first dinner-party. There are a few puzzling things that

One's first dinner-party. trouble him in prospect. He wonders if he should wear gloves, as ladies do, taking them off at the dinner-table. Let me set his mind at rest on this small point, at once. He need not wear

Gloves not worn by men. gloves. In fact, he must not. Another little matter to be remembered is that a quarter of an hour's grace is always understood in dinner invitations. Should the hour indicated be 8 o'clock, then care must be taken to time the arrival at five or ten minutes past the hour. But it is better to be too early than too late. A want of punctuality at this meal is unpardonable. It is the very height of rudeness, annoying to the host and hostess, displeasing to the guests, and regarded as outrageous by the cook.

Punctuality imperative.

When our young man is shown into the drawing-room, he at once goes up to his hostess, no matter whether there is any one he knows nearer to the door than the lady of the house. This is always a fixed rule, whether it be on the occasion of a call or visit, or on having been invited to a party of any kind. When he has been greeted by his hostess he looks round the room to see if there is any one present whom he knows. If so, he goes up to the ladies first, if there are any of his acquaintance present, and afterwards greets the gentlemen. His host will probably have shaken hands with him immediately after his wife has done so. He will then be told what lady he is to take down to dinner, and be introduced to her, if he does not already know her. He must bow, not shake hands, and make small talk for her during the interval between his introduction and the announcement of dinner.

One's first duty to one's hostess.

Then acquaintances.

Introduction to partner.

58

DINNER-PARTIES.

Here is his first real difficulty. To converse with a perfect stranger is always one of the initial social accomplishments to be learned, and it is not at all an easy thing at first. It needs practice. Ninety men out of every hundred offer a remark upon the weather; but unless there has been something very extraordinary going on in the meteorological line, it is better to avoid this subject if possible. A girl at Ascot said to me one lovely day, "That's the eighth man who has informed me that it's a beautiful day." Up came a ninth with the very same observation, and both she and I felt inclined to titter like very schoolgirls It is far better to start with something more original. It is as well to keep the pronoun "I" in the background just at first. If your partner is as nice as she might be, she will soon give you abundant opportunity for talking about yourself.

Making small talk.

If possible, avoid talking about the weather.

The first person singular not a good topic.

By the way, a man must not at his very first dinner-party expect to be given a pretty girl to take down. He may possibly be so fortunate, but those prizes are usually reserved for men of more experience in social life. The young man has probably been invited to make up the necessary number of men, and an un-

The beginner's partner.

59

married lady of uncertain age or an elderly woman without much claim to consideration will probably fall to his share. However, there is this con-
Compensations. solation, she will be excellent for practising upon.

He would not mind making small mistakes so much as if his partner were a young and charming girl. Nor is the art of making small talk so difficult as it would be with
The small-talk art not so difficult. a pair of bright and youthful eyes beaming into your own, and confusing you into forgetfulness of all but their own delightful language.

But what to talk about is the puzzle of the moment. I have known a good beginning made with some
A good beginning. such remark as, "Do you know everybody here?"
This leads perhaps to the acquisition of some information as to the other guests. At table there will be more to suggest topics. The floral decorations often lead up to conversa-
Some useful topics. tion. The colours of the flowers remind one of pictures, and the lady on one's right may be asked if she has been to any exhibitions that may be open. If so, what pictures she liked best. Does she paint? Has she read the novel of the hour? What she thinks of it? Does she bike? At this rate our novice gets on swimmingly, and may safely be left to himself.

I must not omit some small details dealing with the guest on his arrival, and on his way afterwards from the drawing- to the dining-room. The servant who admits him takes his overcoat and hat, either in the hall or in a room set apart for the purpose. Should he be accompanied by a lady he follows her upstairs, and she enters the room slightly in advance of him, probably about a yard or so. The young man must not have the appearance of hanging back, however. He walks steadily and rather briskly up the room.

A few details.

On arrival.

The lady precedes her escort.

When the move to the dining-room is made, the gentlemen offer to the ladies the arm which will place them on the wall side of the staircase, thus avoid-the contact of their dresses with the balusters. But should the dining-room be, as it very frequently is, on the same floor as the drawing-room, then the right arm is offered. The lady sits on the right of her escort at table. The servants usually indicate the seats that the guests are to occupy. Sometimes the host, previously instructed by the hostess, comes to the rescue with, "Your seat is here, I believe, Mr. So-and-so," who immediately takes his lady to the chair on the right of the two the couple are to occupy. The system of name-cards

Taking down to dinner.

Positions at table.

is observed in some circles, but it is not a good one. It is distressing, in

Name-cards. these days of short sight and small rooms, to see several couples wandering about endeavouring to decipher the names on the small cards. It is much better for the host to have made himself master

The better plan. of the order in which the guests are to be seated, and as he enters the dining-room first with the lady of highest social importance, he is ready to point out their places to each couple as they enter.

The first thing to be done on sitting down is to unfold the table napkin and place it across the knee.

Preliminaries at table. The menu is then consulted, and a mental note made of any favourite dish, so that it may not be refused. But all the time a flow of small talk must be kept up with one's partner of the hour. Sometimes she turns to talk with the man on her right. Then her escort may converse with the lady on his left, if she is dis engaged. But he must always re- member that his first duty is to her whom he took down.

There will probably be three or four wineglasses on our young friend's right. One of these—either

The wine- glasses. a long-stemmed, wide- cupped glass or a small tumbler — is for champagne. The coloured glass is for hock, the slenderest and smallest is for sherry, and the claret-glass occupies in dimensions a midway between those of the champagne and sherry-glass.

With regard to the knives and forks, everything is now made very easy for the novice by the way in which the table is laid. The tablespoon is for soup, which must be eaten from the side of the spoon close to the point. The fish knife and fork are placed outside the others, so as to be ready to the hand, the fish course coming directly after the soup. The dishes are usually all handed round at dinner-parties, the carving being done at the sideboard or in an immediately adjoining room, but sometimes the host carves the joint and game.

Knives and forks.

Taking soup.

Carving.

There is occasionally a subtle reason for this preference, not wholly unconnected with a taste for those morsels that especially appeal to the gourmand. The host may desire to secure these for some special, appreciative guest—or for himself ! In some families the principal dishes are always placed before the master of the house to be carved. Maidservants can rarely carve well, and butlers have gone considerably out of fashion in the upper middle classes of society of late years.

When offered the usual choice of dishes or wines, the guest must decide at once and indicate his choice without delay. Any hesitation gives him the

air of being unable to reject either
of being in the position,

Choice of dishes and wines. with regard to food, occupied by the poet who
wrote—

" How happy could I be with either,
Were t'other dear charmer away !"

So he must be prompt, and, should the
dish be handed round, help himself
without delay.

On this very point of helping himself I have seen young men endure
excruciating agonies of shy-

Helping oneself. ness. Sometimes they take
the merest morsel of some
excellent dish, though they would like
very well to have some more. At other
times they help themselves to far too
much, because they are so confused
that they will not take the necessary
time to separate for their own share a
moderate quantity. Occasionally they
drop the spoon or fork with a clatter
into the dish, after which they look
intensely miserable for ten minutes or
so.

The best way to avoid all this is to
preserve absolute self-possession by re-
flecting that the other guests

A useful reflection. are all too well occupied
to pay any attention to such
trifling matters. The self-consciousness of which shyness is the outward and
visible sign, makes a young man feel
that every one is observing him, especially when he is awkward in handling

things. But he may console himself with the conviction that he is of much less importance to them than their own dinner, to say nothing of the ladies who sit beside them.

When asked to choose between claret or hock, he may either mention one or indicate the glass. **The order of the wines.** "Sherry, sir," is the first wine handed round. Then comes the choice between claret and hock. Afterwards "champagne, sir?" **Indicating.** usually answered by slightly drawing the champagne-glass forward, or by a nod; sometimes by a shake of the head. An occasional "Thanks" to the servant is **Thanking servants.** not amiss, but it is unnecessary to keep on expressing gratitude. Some people never dream of saying "Thank you." Others say it out of pure graciousness of manner and gentleness of mind. So our young man may take his choice.

I have observed that when a neat and pretty parlourmaid waits at table she is more likely to be **Maid-servants at table.** thanked than a manservant; and this not only by gentlemen, but by ladies as well. I offer no explanation of why this should be so. I merely record the fact as I have noted it.

The perfection of service resolves itself into absolute accuracy of machinery united to the observant watchfulness of long training. One barely discovers that one needs bread when it is presented at one's elbow. In the same way, vegetables, wine, aërated waters, or whatever one may be drinking, arrive at exactly the right moment. The mechanism or organisation of such waiting is so good that there is no interruption of conversation. The servants understand that a mere turning away from the dish means rejection. Should any guest find a difficulty in helping himself, they simplify matters for him as much as possible.

The perfection of service.

As the dishes are not named when they are handed round, it is necessary to study the menu in order to know what they are. Some young people appear to think that it looks "greedy" to pay much attention to the information given on the dainty little bill of fare; but this, of course, is one of youth's delusions. I have seen a short-sighted young man straining his eyes in the endeavour to read furtively the names of the dishes on his menu. He would have done far better if he had boldly taken it up in his hand to examine it.

Studying the menu.

However hungry one may be, the duty of keeping up a conversation must not be neglected. The viands must never be chosen as a topic, for either praise or blame. If one knows a girl very well, one may ask, "Do you like

A topic to be avoided.

66

sweets ?" or some such question, but it is safer with strangers to avoid the subject of the food provided.

It is scarcely necessary to remark that drinking too much wine is a very bad phase of ill manners.

Moderation in wines. At one time it was actually fashionable to become intoxicated after dinner, but those days are gone, I am thankful to say. The young man who exceeds in this way is soon made aware of the fact that he has given his hostess dire offence. He is never invited again, or not for a long time.

The wineglass is never drained at a draught in polite society ; nor is it considered polite to eat very quickly.

The knife, fork, and spoon are handled as noiselessly as possible. Scraping the edge of the

As little noise as possible. knife against the plate is unpardonable. It produces a grating noise that is excessively unpleasant. In sending a plate away to be replenished, the diner leaves his knife and fork or his spoon, as the case may be, upon it.

In dealing with bread, use neither knife nor fork. It must be broken with the fingers. There is

Bread must be broken. a story of an absent-minded and short-sighted prelate who, with the remark, "My bread, I think ?" dug his fork into the white hand of a lady who sat beside him. He had been badly brought up, or he would not have used his fork, and the white hand would have experienced nothing worse than a sudden grasp.

It requires some expertness and practice for a man with a moustache to take soup in a perfectly

The moustache and soup. inoffensive manner. The accomplishment is worth some trouble.

Some men, who should know better (and some women, too), forget that the mouth should be kept

The mouth. closed while mastication is going on. This is a very important matter. Nature teaches us to keep the mouth open, as any one may see from the way in which children and uncultivated persons eat, but good manners enjoin upon us that to adopt the natural mode is to disgust

Nature not a good guide in this matter. and annoy those with whom we sit at meat. If these little things have not been learned in childhood, it is difficult to master them afterwards. Mothers should also teach their boys (and girls) never to speak while food is in the mouth, and never to drink until it is quite empty. Who would not be mortified if he were to choke ignominiously at the dinner-table ?

The correct way to eat a curry is with a spoon and fork ; but this is the only meat dish that is eaten in this

How to eat a curry, &c. way. Sweetbreads and many other entrées are eaten with the fork alone. It is then held in the right hand. Should a knife be found necessary it can, of course, be used. Vegetable entrées are always eaten with a fork, held in the right hand. Fish is eaten with a silver (or plated) knife and fork. Sauces are never taken very plentifully. The sauce ladle, filled, will be generally

Taking Sauces.

sufficient. I once saw a man, in helping himself to oyster sauce, look scrutinisingly in the sauce-boat and carefully fish about for as many oysters as he could collect in the ladle. This caused some covert amusement, except, perhaps, to the last persons to whom the sauce was handed. They probably found few oysters.

Bread, biscuits, olives, asparagus, celery, and bonbons are the forms of food that may be touched

Foods touched with the fingers.

with the fingers. There used once to be a rule that a bone might be picked, if only the finger and thumb were used in holding it. But that was in the days when table cutlery was far from having been brought to its present condition of perfection. There is now no excuse for handling bones—knives and forks suffice ; and it is only in the lowest grades of society that they are found inadequate.

In helping oneself to salad, it must be placed on the crescent-shaped plate

Salads.

laid down for that purpose before it is handed round. This plate is put at the left side of the round plate. Both knife and fork are often necessary with salads, but if they are sent to table as they should be, with the lettuce and other vegetables broken small, the fork is quite sufficient. It is always disagreeable to see a steel knife used with vinegar, and it should be avoided whenever possible to do so. Oysters served on the shell

Oysters.
are eaten with a fish-knife and fork. Other fish hors d'œuvres are eaten with a fish-fork. It is not always possible to tell, either from the appearance or name of the hors d'œuvre, whether it consists of fish or meat. In that case it is

Hors
d'œuvres.
safer to use an ordinary fork ; and for this reason : the fish-knife has been laid for a fish course, and if it should have been previously unnecessarily used for the hors d'œuvre, it will be needful for the servant to bring another. Fish rissoles may be eaten with a fish-fork only—in fact, any preparation that does not need the knife.

It is a safe rule never to use either

A safe rule.
knife or spoon if the fork will do. With ice-pudding or ices in any form a small spoon is used.

Now let us take the dinner from the very beginning, and go through the

The courses
seriatim.
courses. First, there may be hors d'œuvres, small morsels of various kinds which are found ready to hand when

the guests sit down. I have already referred to these. Next comes soup, generally one thick and one clear. The attendant offers the diner a choice, and he must promptly make it. When it is set before him he begins at once, not waiting till every one is served. He takes up the tablespoon, placed ready at his right hand, and it is not considered very good form to immediately put some salt into the soup before tasting it. People who pride themselves on the possession of a clever cook sometimes feel annoyed at the distrust of her powers shown in this simple action.

Hors d'œuvres.

Soup.

Taste before salting.

With soup small addenda are often handed. The guest helps himself to these, whether they are croûtons, fried bread-crumbs or other supplementary provision, with the spoon handed round on the dish.

The addenda to soup.

It is a very old-fashioned piece of good manners to wait till every one is served. So old-fashioned is it that it survives at present only among the uncultured classes. The correct thing to do nowadays is to begin eating without reference to others. The old style must not only have been trying in consequence of seeing one's food grow cold before one's eyes, but it must

When to begin dining.

71

also have been responsible for making dinner a very slow and tedious meal. Now the attendants remove the plates from the guests first helped directly the fork is laid down, and this greatly accelerates the service.

The soup-plate, if tilted at all, is raised at the side nearest the eater, so that the soup collects at the furthest point from him. It is generally unnecessary to tilt the plate, however. But the thing to avoid is passing the left hand round it in a half-embrace and tilting it towards the eater. This is highly incorrect ; it is also dangerous. The soup has been known to spill on the cloth, and even over the diner.

Tilting the soup-plate.

The direction of the tilt.

When the servant is removing your soup-plate he will sometimes ask, "Any more, sir ?" to which you must reply in the negative. A shake of the head will suffice. Soup is never helped twice. Nor is fish. This is the next course. Bread is always eaten with fish. I have already explained that a silver knife and fork are used. The sauce handed is almost invariably accepted. Sometimes the cruet is handed round, containing some sort of condiment suitable to the fish served. It is, of course, a matter of choice whether this be accepted or not.

Neither soup nor fish may be helped twice.

Fish and fish sauce.

Very few diners work straight through

a menu without omitting some dishes.

Omitting dishes. The idea of giving so many is that there may be some to suit all tastes. No one is expected to take of all, though it is quite permissible to do so.

After the soup and fish the entrées are handed round. The dishes are

Entrées. presented at the left side of the diner, and he helps himself with his right hand, a table-spoon being placed on the dish for that purpose ; or with both hands, using spoon and fork, should the nature of the dish render this necessary.

When slices from a joint, or game, or poultry are handed round, the vege-

Accompaniments to dishes. tables, gravies, and sauces accompanying them are handed after. It is usual to wait for these etceteras before beginning upon the meat, fowl, venison, or game. For instance, no one would commence upon a slice of roast beef or mutton without potatoes or gravy, nor upon a piece of pheasant without browned bread-crumbs, or bread sauce, or gravy. I say "no one" would do it, but I have seen it done, whether in absence of mind or from pressure of appetite I cannot pretend to say. It is a mistake, however.

Sweets and cheese. Cheese is handed round after the sweets in order to prepare the palate for the enjoyment of dessert wines. This, at

73

least, was the original meaning of introducing it at this stage of the meal.

Ice-pudding. But now ice-pudding, when served, follows it, thus contradictorily re-establishing the reign of sweets. Savouries are handed round

Savouries. with the cheese course. These are eaten with a fork. Even a cheese fondu is eaten with a fork, though the cook occasionally fails to bring it to the requisite firmness of consistency, in which case it looks more suited to a spoon ; but the fork must

Celery. do. Celery is eaten with the fingers, like asparagus. This last-named, by the way, if too much cooked, and consequently very

Asparagus. soft and unmanageable, may be eaten with the fork, but must not be touched with the knife. And again, should asparagus be served with the melted butter thrown over it, it must be eaten with a fork. It very seldom is so served, but I have met with this mode in some houses.

Cheese straws are eaten with the fingers. Cheese itself is handed round

Cheese, how served. on a dish or plate with the pieces cut ready to one's hand. The diner helps himself with the knife laid ready beside the pieces of cheese, not with his own knife. If watercress is handed round,

Cheese, how eaten. it is taken up in the fingers and eaten in the same way. Cheese is cut in small pieces and conveyed to the mouth on a piece of bread or biscuit. Very few persons continue to eat it in the old-fashioned way by carrying it to the mouth with the knife. I have seen it taken up with the fingers, but as cheese is apt to smell rather strongly it is better to avoid touching it.

With regard to sweets, it is a safe rule to use the fork only when it suffices for the work in hand. **A safe rule with sweets.** With tarts, as a rule, both spoon and fork are necessary, especially when there is syrup. Cold tart can often be comfortably eaten with a fork. Jellies and creams are eaten with a fork only ; ice-pudding with an ice-spoon, or, failing that, a teaspoon.

From the moment one has unfolded one's napkin and placed the bread it contained at one's left, there is nothing more to do that concerns the " cover," as the preparation for each diner's convenience is called, until the dessert-plate, with its d'oyley, finger-glass, silver knife and fork—and perhaps ice-plate and spoon in addition—is set down before one. Before the **Placing the dessert knife and fork.** ices or dessert are handed round, one must place the dessert-knife and fork at right and left, respectively, of one's plate, and, taking up the finger-glass carefully in one hand, with **D'oyley and finger-glass.** the other place the d'oyley on the cloth to the left of one's plate, then setting the finger-glass down upon it. I say "carefully," because these glasses are often of the lightest possible kind, and are occasionally of a costly description. Besides, rough handling might tend to spill the water they contain.

With regard to the dessert fruits, &c., there are a few puzzles to be found among them for the inexperienced. Grapes present one of these. They are taken up singly, and afterwards the skin and seeds have to be expelled as unobtrusively as possible. It is a matter of great difficulty to accomplish this by any other method than using the hand, therefore this is the accepted custom. The forefinger is curved above the mouth in a manner which serves to conceal the ejectment, and the skin and seeds are in this way conveyed to the plate, the fingers being afterwards wiped with the napkin. Bananas are peeled with the knife and fork, and the pieces are conveyed to the mouth by means of the fork. Oranges are cut in two, then in four, and with the aid of knife and fork the contents of each section are extracted in two or more parts, and carried to the lips on the fork. Apples and pears are peeled with the knife and fork ; peaches, apricots, and nectarines in the same way.

Strawberries are taken by the stem,

Dessert.

Grapes.

Expelling skin and seeds.

Bananas.

Oranges.

Apples and pears, &c.

dipped in sugar and cream, and carried to the lips with the fingers.

Strawberries. If the fruit has been picked free of husks and stem, it may be bruised on the plate with sugar and cream, and eaten with a spoon. Preserved ginger is eaten with the knife and fork.

A spoon is necessary with pines, melons, and very juicy strawberries, after they have been prepared with the knife and fork.

Pines and melons.

Nuts are cracked with the nut-crackers, and then extracted by the fingers. With filberts and Brazil nuts the knife and fork are called into requisition in order to free them from skin, but walnuts are too intricate for anything less wonderful in mechanism than the human hand. In view of this, they are sometimes prepared before being sent to table, and of late years they have been sold ready cracked and peeled for this purpose.

Nuts.

Almonds are never sent to table in their shells, so that they present no difficulties to the novice. At dessert they are usually accompanied by raisins, which, like the almonds, are carried to the mouth in the fingers.

Almonds.

Crystallised fruits are cut with the knife and fork, unless they happen to be of a small size, such as cherries. In that

Crystallised fruits.

77

case they are eaten whole, being carried to the lips on the fork.

Liqueurs are handed round at dessert, poured out ready into the small glasses that are called after

Liqueurs.

them. There is generally a choice, such as "Chartreuse or Bénèdictine, sir?" to which it is unnecessary to reply, "Both, please," as a historic young man did once.

The servants often leave the dining-room when the dessert is placed on the table, and when this is so, the wine is passed round from hand to hand, each

Passing the wines.

gentleman attending first to the lady he has escorted and then helping himself before passing on the decanter, claret jug, or champagne bottle. The good old fashion of using silver decanter-stands has long disappeared, to the detriment of many a good tablecloth. So has the genial and hospitable fashion of drinking wine with one's guests, and they with each other. But this may be rather a good thing in the interests of temperance.

Apropos to this subject, I may remark that there is now nothing singular in drinking nothing but water.

The water-drinker not singular.

The days are gone when a man was thought a milksop because he could not " drink his bottle," or if he refused wine or spirits. Should any young man prefer water, he asks for it when the servants offer him wine. He is then offered

Apollinaris or distilled water or soda-water, or some other preparation of filtered and distilled water, and may choose some of these in preference to plain water.

Claret is the favourite dessert wine of the day, but port is still seen at some tables, and it is usual to offer champagne, as many prefer to drink only one kind of wine throughout the meal, from start to finish. In fact, this is becoming quite a fashion in some sets. The host provides cigars and cigarettes for his guests, and it would not be necessary or advisable to produce one's own supply.

"One wine" diners.

Cigars and cigarettes.

When the ladies rise to leave the dining-room, the gentleman who sits nearest the door opens it for them, and stands beside it until they have all passed through, when he closes it after them. However anxious he may be to join them in the drawing-room, he must not do so until the others make a move. Sometimes, if he is very young and rather "out of it" when politics or sport are under discussion, his host says to him, " I'm afraid you are bored. If you would like to join the ladies, don't stand on ceremony." But on the other hand he may dread the ordeal of entering the drawing-room alone, and feel that the safer way is to wait for a convoy. This he must decide for himself.

When the ladies leave the dining-room.

Perhaps his host may wish to talk confidentially with some other guest. If he makes this apparent to the younger man, the latter must accept any such intimation as the above, understanding it to be a courteous mode of dismissing him.

A hint from the host.

The ordinary rule is that the gentlemen join the ladies all together, the man of highest position leaving the dining-room first, the host last. Tea is then carried round in the drawing-room, and the gentlemen take the empty cups from the ladies and put them down in some safe place, out of the way of risk of accident. Should any lady sing or play, the gentleman nearest to her escorts her to the piano and helps her to arrange her music, to dispose of her gloves, fan, handkerchief, &c.

The ordinary rule when rejoining the ladies.

When a lady sings or plays.

It is scarcely etiquette for young men to leave first after a dinner-party. It is more usual for the elders of the party to make the first move towards departure. But should the young man have an engagement of a pressing kind, such as a promise to escort ladies to a ball, he must withdraw in good time, explaining the position to his hostess.

Leaving early.

No one leaves after a dinner-party without saying "Good-night" to his host and hostess. Even in the case of

an early departure, before the gentlemen have left the dining-room, the
guest must visit the drawing-room to
make his adieux, not only to the lady
of the house, but to any others who
may be of his acquaintance. Those
whom he has met for the first time
that evening may be saluted with a
parting bow.

At a formal dinner-party the evening
suit is imperative, with dress-coat,
white or black waistcoat, black
trousers, and white tie. When dining
with friends with whom one is on
terms of familiarity, the dinner-jacket
may be substituted for the coat. Black
ties often take the place of white.
Patent-leather shoes or boots must be
worn. It would be unpardonable to
appear in thick walking-boots or
shoes ; and the necessity for immaculately polished footgear has cost the
young man of the present day many
a cab. His varnished shoes must
show no trace of mud or dust. To
tell the truth, he often carries a silk
handkerchief in his pocket wherewith
to obliterate the traces of the latter.

The pocket-handkerchief used with
evening dress must be of white
cambric, and of as good a colour as
one's washerwoman will permit. It
ought to be of fine quality. The hair
must be short and very well brushed.

It used to be the custom to tip the
servants on leaving the house where
one had dined as a guest, but this has

fallen into disuse. There are many
men who hand a silver coin to the
butler, or footman, or waiting-maid
who helps them into their coats, calls
up their carriage, or hails a cab for
them, seeing them into it, or rendering
any other service of a similar kind.
This is a matter that each man must
decide for himself. It is only necessary to remark that the custom of
giving shillings or half-crowns to the
servants after a dinner-party no longer
reigns ; though there are always good-
natured folk who will not let it abso
lutely die out.

PUBLIC DINNERS.

THE following information is supplied
by a gentleman well-known in the City,
and thoroughly *au fait* in

**Public
dinners.**

such matters.

"Public dinners may be
classed as those given by associations,
or public bodies, and those given by
institutions, such as some of the great
City companies. When given by an
association, the function is

**When given
by an
association.**

generally managed by a
committee, who have the
arrangement of all the
details, such as choosing the menu,
the wines, preparing the programme
of music, instrumental or vocal, and
arranging the due sequence of the
speeches. A guest invited to such an
entertainment who may not be of the
few highly placed personages who sit
at the cross-table or on the daïs, and
from whom speeches are expected,

On arrival.

will, on arriving at the hall,
hotel, or public institution
selected, find that the first thing required
of him will be his invitation card. In
exchange for this he will be handed
a more or less elaborate menu card,
which will also contain the list of music

and a sketch showing the positions of the guests' seats at the tables. After depositing his hat and overcoat in the cloak-room, receiving a numbered ticket for them, he enters the reception- or drawing-room, his name is announced, and he passes into the room, goes up to the members of the com-

Saluting the hosts. mittee, who stand by themselves to receive the guests, bows or shakes hands, and passes on to join the other guests who are either sitting or standing in groups engaged in conversation. When dinner

When dinner is announced. is announced the hosts and the highest in rank of the guests file into the dining-room and take up their position by their chairs, followed by the rest ; any clergyman present says grace on being asked to do so, and the banquet commences. Strangers sitting next to each other soon fall into conversation, and after the dispatch of the solid portion

The order of the ceremony. of the repast come the speeches. Music is played at intervals, perhaps a few songs sung by professionals, then dessert, cigars, and coffee, after which the guests find their way to the drawing-room for more general conversation, some preferring to leave without re-entering the drawing-room. In such large gatherings it is not necessary to take leave of the hosts, as a rule.

" Dinners given by City companies are very much on the same principle.

The guest has but to don his evening clothes and carry himself with easy composure, not always quite a simple matter to the inexperienced, if one may judge from the hurried steps and the sudden bob that many give on entering the reception - room after arrival."

Dinners given by City companies.

At dinners given on behalf of charities, it is well to go prepared with a subscription, as a collection is often made on these occasions. If not prepared to subscribe, it is more discreet to stay away.

Dinners for charities.

With regard to tips the only ones really recognised are those for which the plates on the cloak-room table are laid ready in expectation of small silver coins. Though no fees are actually necessary at table, the initiated person is well aware that the man behind his chair can administer to his wants and see that he is liberally provided with viands and wines or other matters without keeping him waiting longer than necessary. A tip, quietly conveyed before the dinner is under way, is not by any means wasted.

On tips.

It sometimes happens that semi-official dinners are given at private houses, when proprietors of newspapers or wealthy men interested in certain undertakings, entertain the staff of those employed. In such circum-

Semi-official dinners at private houses.

stances it may be as well to warn the guests against addressing the footmen as "waiter." This may appear to be superfluous advice, but I have myself been present when the mistake was made, evidently to the intense indignation of the magnificent being thus addressed.

At such dinners as these, the host treats his guests as his social equals for the nonce. By having invited them to his house he places himself in the position of regarding them as he would his own friends at his dinner-table. Any infraction of this would be in the worst taste. It is also usual to abstain from any business talk at such times as these, the conversation being encouraged to dwell on general topics.

Though the fiction of social equality is maintained by the host, the guests need not adopt a familiar, free-and-easy manner in response. True manliness involves sufficient self-respect to preserve the possessor from falling into this error ; but it is, perhaps, a little difficult for the novice, on such occasions, to bear himself in such wise as to avoid undue familiarity on one hand and an air of stiffness and stand-offishness on the other. In his anxiety not to appear to presume upon the friendliness of his host's manner, he is apt to wear a rather repellent air. And this is more particularly so when the *employé* is by birth the equal, if not the superior, of his entertainer. It often happens that a man at the head of a great business has risen from obscure beginnings to the command of wealth and a high position in the world, enjoying a title and many of the extraneous advantages of rank. Among those whom he employs may be several who are his social superiors in all but wealth ; but any of them who imagine that this fact gives them any claim upon his consideration or entitles them to converse with him upon a footing of equality, make a radical mistake Their position, as regards their employer, is exactly that justified by their standing in his firm. The true gentleman is well aware of this, and would never dream of asserting himself in any way on the strength of being well-born or highly educated. He leaves all that kind of thing to the man who feels his claim to gentlemanhood to be so shadowy and insecure as to need constant insistance.

Besides, the host is usually the elder, and deference to seniority is an important part of good manners, and sits extremely well upon the young.

WHEN accompanying ladies who express a wish for refreshment, it is

Should ladies request refreshment. not necessary to select a very expensive restaurant or confectioner's. One suitable to the social status of the party should be chosen. The young man must pay for what his

The man pays. companions eat and drink, and very often this is a most embarrassing matter. He may have enough money in his pocket to defray the bill, and he may not. In any case, he is often unable to afford it,

Though he cannot afford it. but the probabilities are that if he has the wherewithal about him, he will pay in order to extricate himself from an awkward predicament, even though he may consequently be crippled financially for some days to come. If he has only two or three shillings in his pocket, he feels extremely uncomfortable. No

No well-bred woman would make the request. well-bred woman or girl would ever place an acquaintance on the horns of such a dilemma. But unfortunately there are many girls and women who are lacking in taste and refinement, and who would regard it as an excellent joke to play such a trick upon a "fellow," as they would probably call him, and enjoy his discomfort.

The best thing to do in such a case is to be perfectly frank and open. "I'm extremely sorry, but I have not sufficient cash with me for the purpose." It is very disagreeable to have **The best course to adopt.** to say so, but it is less mortifying than to have to acknowledge it to the waiter at the restaurant. A young man told me that he had once, in such a case, to leave the table on pretence of speaking to the proprietor and fly round to a pawnbroker's to pledge his watch.

A really well-bred girl or woman **A well-bred girl would bear her own expenses.** would make it clear that she intended to pay for her own meal, and that only on that condition would she accept the escort of the young man.

Sometimes after a run on a bicycle or a hot walk, a young man will say to his sister and her friend, "Come **On taking advantage of a man's generosity.** in and have an ice." If the friend is one of the unscrupulous sort, she will very probably run him into what, for him, is a considerable expense. He must pay it, however, and the worst of it is that he cannot sit there and let her eat all by herself. Even his sister, should she be present, must in good manners join in to a certain extent. Otherwise the implied reproof would be too obvious for good breeding

AT LUNCH.

LUNCHEON is a comparatively informal meal. The guests do not pair off, as at dinner, but on the meal being announced the host, if there be one, would open the door for the ladies, who would go downstairs, followed by the hostess, the gentlemen behind her. Very often the master of the house is absent at luncheon, in which case the hostess would rise, and, addressing her principal guest, would propose to her to lead the way downstairs. "Shall we go down to lunch, Mrs. So-and-so?" would be sufficient. The other ladies would probably be sufficiently versed in the laws of society to refrain from preceding those of higher position, and the hostess would always be the last lady to leave the drawing-room. The guests sit down where they please, the host or hostess sometimes making a suggestion on the matter.

Going down to luncheon.

In the absence of the host.

Positions at table.

After the meal the guests return to the drawing-room, but only for a short time. The gentlemen resume their overcoats and take their hats and umbrellas in the

After the meal.

hall, where they had left them. Should a man make a call at luncheon-time, he is often asked to remain for the meal. In that case he would carry his hat and stick into the dining-room with him, just as he would if making an ordinary call. But it is much better never to call anywhere at lunch-time unless one is on very familiar terms with the family. Many young men acquire a reputation for "cadging" for lunch or dinner in this way.

Making calls at luncheon-time.

Invitations from the younger members of the family are not official, unless plainly endorsed by the elders, or one of them. "Miss Lucy invited me to lunch" is a poor plea. "Frank asked me to come and dine this evening," is no better. Young men cannot be too particular about this matter. "I'll get my mother to ask you to dinner, old man," would be the safer sort of invitation. The lady of the house must fix the date, and she usually writes the invitation herself or gives it personally.

Invitations from young members of the family.

Should a daughter of the house give a young man an invitation to any meal, without reference to her father or mother, it would be incorrect in the highest degree to accept it. As to children, their invitations go for nothing, of course, though cases have been known in which they have

Unendorsed invitations from a daughter of the house.

been accepted. " I met little Eddy in the park, and he made me come in with him." This has a very poor and pitiable sound at luncheon hour or tea-time.

It is not necessary to make one's adieux to each guest in turn. The hostess is taken leave of **Making one's adieux.** first, as a rule, and the lady, or ladies, with whom one has been conversing will expect a special word and bow, perhaps offering a hand ; but a general bow will be sufficient for those to whom one is not very well known. It is only at family parties that one has conscientiously to go round the room shaking hands with everybody.

GENTLEMEN are in great request at five o'clock tea. Their duties are rather onerous if there are *Duties of men at five o'clock tea.* but one or two men and the usual crowd of ladies. They have to carry teacups about, hand sugar, cream, and cakes or muffins, and keep up all the time a stream of small talk, as amusing as they can make it. They must rise every time a lady enters or leaves the room, opening the door for her exit if no one else is nearer to it, and, if the hostess requests them, they must see the lady downstairs to her carriage or cab.

With regard to the viands, a man helps himself, but not till he has seen that all the ladies in his *His own refreshment.* vicinity have everything they can possibly want. His hostess, or some lady deputed by her to preside at the tea-table, gives him tea or coffee, and he adds sugar and cream.

With regard to afternoon at-homes, the arrangements are quite *Afternoon at-homes.* different. Invitations are sent out a fortnight or three weeks before, generally the latter, and in the height of the season even longer.

Suppose the young man's name to be Edward Smith. His invitation would be as follows :—

MR. EDWARD SMITH.

LADY DART

At Home,

Tuesday, November 3rd.

4 to 7.

12, Evergreen Square.

R. S. V. P.

He replies, on a sheet of note-paper :—" Mr. Edward Smith has much pleasure in accepting Lady Dart's kind invitation for Tuesday afternoon, November 3rd."

Accepting invitation.

It's a great mistake to write :—" Will have much pleasure in accepting." Accepting is the action of the present moment while he is writing the reply. "Will have" refers to the future, and is therefore unsuitable. The answering of invitations is a simple matter enough, but it is a test of good breeding.

A great mistake.

AT THE PLAY.

At a theatre the underbred man is often in evidence, not only in the low-priced seats, bu also all over the house. He has been seen—and heard—in private boxes.

The under-bred man at the play.

A well-known music-hall celebrity administered a scathing reproof to one of these, who persisted in talking loudly while she was singing. Stopping short, she looked up at the box in which he sat, and cried : "One fool at a time, please," after which he was as quiet as a mouse. It is a piece of bad manners to enter the theatre late, disturbing the audience and annoying the players or singers. It is equally rude to leave before the entertainment is ended, unless the interval be chosen when nothing is going on.

Entering late.

And leaving early.

At a concert this is particularly true, for there are devotees of music who hang upon every note and to whom it is a distinct loss to miss a single phrase of the compositions they have come to hear. Singers, actors, and actresses generally possess the sensitive, sympathetic, artistic temperament, and it is wounding to them to see

Inattention uncivil.

members of the audience fidgeting,
rustling about, chattering, laughing, and
otherwise showing inattention when
they are doing their best to entertain
them. It is, therefore, uncivil to betray
inattention. A little appreciation goes
a long way with the members of the
professions of music and
the drama. An actor told
me once that after having
made a certain speech two or three
times without any sign of amusement
from the audience, on the fourth night
of the play a single silvery note of
musical mirth was heard from the
stalls. It was but one note—say E flat
on the treble clef—but the audience
immediately joined in, perceiving the
point of the speech as though it had
been illuminated for them by this one
little laugh. He declared that ever
after that night his formerly unsuccess-
ful "lines" elicited a roar of laughter.
Probably this was partly due to the
sense of encouragement he felt, in-
spiring him to due emphasis.

On
appreciation.

In taking ladies to a place of entertainment a gentleman hands them
into their carriage, a cab, or
an omnibus, getting in last.
Arrived at their destination
the gentleman alights first,
handing out the ladies, and giving any
necessary orders to the coachman, or
paying the cabman's fare. By the way,
it is always as well to give instructions
to the coachman about where he is to

In taking
ladies to a
place of enter-
tainment.

be found, and at what hour he is to pick up his party, before entering the carriage, as policemen view with much disfavour any prolonged dialogue outside a place of entertainment where vehicles are setting down their occupants in quick succession. Should there be a footman, of course all these difficulties are obviated, as he can carry the instructions to the coachman, and also knows where to find the carriage when the performance is over.

Instructions to the coachman.

Should a hired brougham be used as a conveyance in going to any place of entertainment, or even a party at a private house, it is an excellent plan to give the coachman a bright-coloured handkerchief, scarlet or orange perhaps, that he may wear it conspicuously displayed, and can in this way be at once recognised. It is a miserable business on a wet night to hunt for a brougham up and down ill-lighted streets when in evening dress and patent leather boots, and anything that tends to shorten the task is advisable. Nor do ladies enjoy waiting in the draughty vestibule of opera-house, theatre, or concert-room for an indefinite period while a short-sighted cavalier is groping about the streets for their carriage.

Should a hired brougham be used.

To obviate waiting.

If it is a question of a cab, the commissionaire at the door is the best person to get one, which he will do for a small fee.

Here again a word of warning is needed. There are men who, in their special care of the ladies in their charge, forget that it is no part of the duty of a gentleman to ignore the claims of other women who have not the advantage of belonging to their party. I have seen men who ought to have known better rudely pushing other ladies away from the door of a cab or railway carriage in order that their own womenkind may be well looked after. It is all very well to be attentive and anxious to do one's best, but it is ill-bred to the last degree to subject to rudeness any ladies who happen to be without a gentleman to look after them.

A word of warning.

Considera-tion due to all women.

Retribution followed very swiftly in one instance of the kind. At Sandown station one day the second special train for Waterloo was coming in, and the platform was crowded with gaily-dressed women, tired and hot after the walk across the fields on a tropical July day. A lady and small Eton boy were together, and suddenly, when about to open the door of a carriage at the moment the train came to a standstill, found them-selves all but thrown down by a sweeping motion of the arm of a young man who was bent on reserving that particular carriage for his party. With

An instance.

out a word of apology to the lady, he shouted to his sisters and friends to "Come on," still holding back the two who had wished to get in. They entered the next compartment, and as they did so the lady remarked to her companion, "What an extremely ill-mannered person that is!" Meanwhile the party next door were settling down and congratulating themselves on having secured seats, when one of them turned to their over-zealous friend and re-marked, "I saw Lady Blank get into the next carriage with her eldest boy." "*Who?*" he asked, with a sudden and remarkable rush of colour on his face. The lady to whom he had behaved so rudely turned out to be one from whom he had that very morning received a long-desired invitation to spend a few days at her country house in the following month. This he owed to the good offices of a friend in the F. O., and, delighted at having made such a step in his social career, he had at once written off accepting the invita-tion. It is scarcely necessary to add that he never made the visit, but had to wire at the last moment one of those conventional excuses that the "unco guid" call fibs, but which are only the transparent devices adopted by society to lubricate some of the more difficult of its processes.

Between the acts of a play the modern man thinks it his duty to himself to go out and have a drink perhaps smoke a cigarette. There was a time when, had any such suggestion been made to a gentleman **The interval.** who had constituted himself the escort of a lady, he would have asked, though perhaps not in Milton's words—

"And leave thy fair side all unguarded, lady?"

But now the majority of young men visit the bar or the *foyer*. But who shall say what golden opinions are won by those who do not follow the custom, who refrain from acquiring the odour of tobacco, or whiskey, or **How a man may win golden opinions.** brandy while they are in the company of ladies in the heated atmosphere of a theatre? A lady sometimes says to the men of her party, "I see that there is a general stampede going on. Don't mind me if you would like to go out." If they go she thinks, "Oh, they are just like the rest." If they stay she says to her own heart, "How delightful it is to find a man who can do without a B.-and-S. or a smoke for two or three hours!" and up they go many pegs in her estimation.

Apart from the lady he is with and considerations connected with her, there is the inconvenience **Other considerations.** to which many of the audience are subjected by the passing in and out of so many. However, it is a recognised custom, so much so that a smoking *foyer* is attached to all the best theatres, and a warning bell is rung in it by the management a few minutes before the rising of the curtain.

Refreshments are frequently carried round by attendants to private boxes, and sometimes in the stalls as well. Should they appear, it is the duty of the gentleman of the party to ask the lady or ladies if they wish for any, and to pay for what is consumed. It is, however, a rare thing for ladies to eat or drink at the play. The gentleman also pays for the programme at the few theatres where a charge is made.

When refreshments are brought around.

I may mention, by the way, that it is not considered very good form to pay for programmes at theatres where the management makes no charge. Instances have been known where attendants have been discharged for accepting such fees ; and even apart from this, it is tantamount to presenting the attendant with sixpence or a shilling if one insists on paying for a programme or two provided free of charge. Many of the attendants are superior to accepting it.

On unnecessary payment for programmes.

AT A BALL.

THE etiquette of the ball-room is not difficult to acquire, and yet there are thousands of young men

The etiquette of the ball-room. going into society constantly who flagrantly fail in it. Their bad manners are conspicuous. They decline to dance unless the prettiest girls in the room are "trotted out" for them, block the doorways, haunt the refreshment-room, and after supper promptly take their leave. Could any course of conduct be in worse taste? And what can a poor hostess do? Young men are necessary at dances, and they must be invited. If they will not dance, who shall make

"The delight of the hostess's heart." them? The delight of the average hostess's heart is the well-bred man, unspoiled by conceit, who can always be depended on to do his duty. He arrives in good time, fills his card before very long, and can be asked to dance with a plain, neglected wallflower or two without resenting it. He takes his partner duly to the refreshment-room after each dance, if she wishes to go, and provides her with whatever she wishes. Before leaving her, he sees her

safe at her chaperon's side. If he should sit out a dance he returns in time to claim his partner for the next, not leaving her till it is half over, as is the wont of some young men. The truth

Self-denial the secret of good society.

is that society demands a never-ending series of self-denying actions from those who belong to it, and the more cheerfully these are performed, the more perfect are the manners. What can be more enjoyable than to sit in some cool retreat with a charming girl, enjoying one of those innocent flirtations that do so much to give zest to life ? But delightful though it be, the temptation to prolong it must be resisted, if an expectant partner is missing her dance and waiting in the ball-room to be claimed.

It is bad manners to go to a ball unless one is accomplished in the art of

Non-dancers should not accept invitations.

dancing. To do so is to take the place of one who may be more expert and therefore in greater request. Consequently, every man who wishes to be a success in society must learn to dance. There are abundant opportunities for doing so at the various dancing "academies," as they are rather unsuitably entitled, for there is not much about them of

The value of private lessons.

the academical, as generally understood. Private lessons are dearer than the others, but they are really necessary for most men who have not been taught to dance when boys. The whole attention of the teacher should be given during the first three or four. A man has so much to learn in addition to the correct movements of his feet. He must be taught to hold his head up, to grasp his partner gently but firmly, not to tread on her toes or knock his knees against hers, and also how to steer his course and hers in an imaginary crowded room. Afterwards come the finishing touches, when, perfect in the steps and carriage of the body, the learner is taught to glide gently from foot to foot, regulating his pace as quickly or as slowly as he may wish. At first this seems to be impossible, for the novice is inclined to " rush his fences," as it were, and he waltzes round the room at breakneck speed, making himself giddy and breathless, and sometimes causing dire catastrophe. A girl finds it difficult to forgive a man who has made her look ridiculous. The fall of a couple is not a frequent occurrence in a ball-room, but when it does happen it is almost always the man's fault. Girls take much more naturally to the graceful movements of the dance, and are, besides, more often taught in childhood than their brothers.

The finishing touches.

A fall generally the man's fault.

At a private ball the guest enters and greets his hostess before speaking to any one else. She shakes hands with

him and passes him on to some one
to introduce him to partners, perhaps
her husband, perhaps her
son. With this beginning he
will probably get on very
well and may half-fill his card, and he
should take care to do so at once, for at
some balls the nice girls are immediately
snapped up and engaged for even the
extras before they have been
twenty minutes in the room.
"Are you engaged for every
dance, Miss Grey? Can you
spare me one?" And Miss Grey
probably gives him one, but if he is
a stranger of whose calisthenic prowess
nothing is known, she is careful to give
him only one. Sometimes his partners,
if they discover that he dances well,
introduce him to their sisters and
friends. If, however, he should find
himself left high and dry towards the
end of the evening, he should go back
to the gentlemen of the house and ask
them to introduce him to somebody else.
Young men of experience in such
matters usually manage very well
without this, but the novice has often
to face the alternative of dancing no
more or asking to be introduced.

Hostesses sometimes make special
introductions for the "supper" dance,
the one immediately preced-
ing that meal. This means
that the man introduced,
unless engaged to dance it
with some one else, is imperatively

At a private ball.

The card should be filled early.

The "supper" dance.

called upon to accept the partner offered him and take her down to supper.

In asking a lady to dance it is usual to say, "Will you give me this waltz?" or "May I have this barn-dance?" Some young men say, "Would you like to dance this? Come along then!" but such a form of address is only suited to intimates.

Asking a lady to dance.

When the dance is over, and the partner left with her friends, the man says, "Thank you," bows, and leaves her.

After the dance:

If he wishes to see any lady to her carriage, he asks her permission to do so, folds her wraps round her, hands her in, and stands until the carriage has gone some yards away.

Seeing a lady to her carriage.

ENGAGEMENT AND MARRIAGE.

THE old-fashioned rule that a man must approach the father of a girl before offering himself in marriage to her has now, to some extent, died out. At the same time it is considered dishonourable for any one to **A man may not propose when her family object.** propose to a girl in the face of the decided disapprobation of her family. Clandestine courtship is also regarded as dishonourable, except in circumstances where the girl is unhappy or oppressed and needs a champion. The usual way to ask for the admired one's hand in marriage is in **Proposal in person.** person. This is always preferable to writing, though some men have not the courage to adopt the first course. Should the lady accept the offer, the happy wooer must take the earliest opportunity of seeing her father, **Asking the father's permission.** or, failing him, her nearest friend, and begging him to permit the engagement. Should he consent, all is well ; but in the contrary case, his decision must be accepted. To allow a girl to engage herself against the wish of her family is to drag her into a false position. Very often submission to the decree effects more towards procuring its reversal than violent opposition. It is difficult, of course, for young people to be patient, but if they can only manage a little of it they would find the truth of the French proverb, "All things come round to those who know how to wait."

Should the father refuse consent.

Immediately upon having the engagement ratified, the accepted suitor gives the lady an engagement ring. This should be as handsome a present as he can afford to buy. Together with all other presents and correspondence on both sides, this ring must be returned if the engagement should be broken off.

The engagement ring.

The accepted man is in duty bound to spend most of his leisure with his intended bride. He must not go off for a sojourn abroad while she is spending some weeks by the sea in England, unless she has expressed a wish to that effect. It would be a considerable "snub" to her to do so. Society has sometimes been amused by the announcement one day of a "marriage having been arranged between Mr. A. and Miss B.," and on the next of the intention of Mr. A. to start for a tour round the world. This almost

One's duty to one's betrothed.

A significant announcement.

always means that the man has been entrapped into a proposal, and would willingly retreat if he honourably could. Such things happen only too often. Manœuvring mothers have much to answer for in the matter. Worldly girls have often sufficient wisdom of the serpent to bring a reluctant wooer to the point and, by immediately announcing the engagement to their friends, to make it extremely difficult for him to retreat.

Sometimes a girl falls so wildly in love with a man that she creates a kind of corresponding, though passing, fervour in him, and while it lasts he believes himself in love, though his emotions are only a mixture of gratified vanity and that physical attraction which needs true love to redeem it from the fleshly sort. Should marriage follow upon such courtships as these, where the girl takes ever the initiative, the union is very seldom a happy one. The wife never feels sure that her husband really loves her or would have chosen her. She knows that he was her choice, rather than she his, and a racking jealousy seizes her and makes her not only miserable herself, but a very uncomfortable companion for him. He, too, often finds when it is too late that she fulfils none of his ideals, and is in many ways a contrast to the girl he would have chosen if she had

When a girl takes the initiative.

The unhappy sequel.

not whirled him into the vortex of her
own strong feeling. And he occasionally wonders if she may not some day
experience a similar strength of attraction for some other man and let herself
be carried away by it as she had been
by her feeling for him. "Hot fires
soon burn out," he thinks, and remem-
bers the warning given to Othello:
"She hath deceived her father, and
may thee." No man should
Long
engagements. drag a girl into a long engagement. Nor should any
man propose to a girl until he is in a
position to provide for her. He is
only standing in the way of other
wooers who may be well supplied with
this world's gear. Such
And trifles as wealth and ease
unsuitable
positions. may appear as nought to the
mind of the youthful lover,
not to be weighed for a moment in the
balance with love and young romance.
The girl, too, may be of the same way
of thinking at the time, but it the more
behoves the man, the stronger, to consider her and to remember
A man's duty that poverty is such a bitter
to look
at cold facts. and a cruel thing that it
even kills love at times.
Recrimination in the home is a hard
thing to bear. And yet how many
millions of women since the world
began have said to their husband:
"Oh, why did I ever marry you? I
could have done so much better."

And how many men have said to

their wives : " Well ! You were determined to have me, so now you must
make the best of me."

However, we will suppose these rocks
and quicksands past, the engaged couple
happy, and the wedding day at hand.

Custom demands that the
bridegroom shall present her
bouquet to the bride, as well
as bouquets and a present
each to the bridesmaids. He must
furnish the house for the bride in every
detail, not excepting the house and
table linen, which, in the old days of
spinning-wheels, was wont to be con-
tributed by the bride herself.

The bridegroom's obligations.

He must provide the wedding ring
and the carriage in which his best man
and himself go to church. He pays
the fees to clergyman and
clerk, but it is the best man
who hands them over. With
him the bridegroom waits at the altar
till the bride arrives. She takes her
place at his left hand for the first time,
and at the proper moment he produces
the ring which is the symbol of their
union.

The best man.

The usual dress of a bridegroom consists of a very dark blue
frock-coat, light trousers,
light or white scarf-tie,
patent boots, and a new hat.

The bridegroom's dress.

DRESS.

It is absolutely true, though in a very limited sense, that the tailor makes the man. If a man does not dress well in society he cannot be a success. If he commits flagrant errors in costume he will not be invited out very much, of that he may be certain. If he goes to a garden party in a frock-coat and straw hat, he is condemned more universally than if he had committed some crime. The evidence of the latter would not be upon him for all men to read, as the evidence of his ignorance in social forms is, in his mistaken notions of dress. Things are more involved than ever in the sartorial line, since so many new sports and pastimes have sprung up for men. A man cannot consult his tailor upon every trifling detail, even if his tailor were always a perfectly reliable authority, which is not always the case, for there are tailors and tailors. A young man's finances do not always allow him to go to one of the best, and the second and third-rate artists in

Importance of dress.

The penalty of solecisms of costume.

Tailors not always to be relied on.

cloth are apt to purvey second and third-rate fashions to their customers.

A brief summary of the forms of dress appropriate to various occasions may be of some use to the inexperienced. It is obvious that to enter into detail would be out of place in a matter where change is the order of the day. But there are **"Certain fixed rules."** certain fixed rules that are, in a sense, permanent, and with these I may succinctly deal.

For morning wear the morning-coat or jacket or the tweed suit is correct. **For morning wear.** After lunch, when in town, the well-dressed man may continue to wear his morning-coat or the regulation frock-coat, with trousers of some neat, striped grey mixture. The tailor's name for the material of these is "mixed cheviots."

Light trousers. It is not considered good form to wear very light trousers except on special occasions, such as weddings, garden parties, or afternoon assemblies of a festive kind. Even then it is better to err on the quiet side than to be overloud. The days of broadcloth have long gone by, and coats are now made **Black coats.** of vicuna cloth or black twilled worsteds, with a dull finish and of an elastic quality. Waistcoats may be single or double-breasted. There is no restriction as to the colour of the tie.

The Park suit may consist of a grey

154

or light-brown frock-coat, with waistcoat and trousers to match,
The Park
suit. and this is the usual dress
for Ascot, the smartest of all
the races. At Sandown the low hat
and tweed suit, or long racing coat, are
worn, except on such days as the Princess of Wales is present, when the
Prince sets the example of wearing a
black coat and silk hat, and all other
men are expected to follow his example.

For a morning walk in the Park in
summer the straw hat, or low hat and
tweed suit, are as correct as
For a summer the black coat and silk hat.
morning in
the Park. But it must be remembered
that a straw hat or low hat
cannot be worn with a black coat of
any kind. The " pot " hat and brown
boots are permissible with an overcoat,
under which there may be a
Brown boots. tweed suit, but brown boots
may not otherwise accompany a black
coat, though they are admissible with
the Ascot suit.

There are special suits for all kinds
of outdoor amusements, such as shooting, golfing, tennis, boating,
Special suits. driving, riding, bicycling,
fishing, hunting, &c., but into the details of these it is unnecessary to enter.
It may be remarked, how-
Spoiling an ever, that it is easy to stultify
otherwise
good effect. the whole effect of these,
however perfectly they may
be " built " by the tailor, by the addi-

tion of a single incongruous article of attire ; such as a silk hat or patent boots with a shooting-suit.

The dress-coat is no longer made of broadcloth, the shiny finish of which would now have a very old-fashioned appearance. The ordinary evening coat is made of an elastic twill cloth, with a dull finish. Its elasticity makes it fit to perfection when cut by a good tailor. Of course it would be incorrect to wear other than black trousers with it. The waistcoat is much cut away, to show a wide expanse of immaculately got-up shirt-front.

The modern dress-coat.

This is the only correct costume for evening wear on all occasions of a formal nature. The dinner-jacket has very largely superseded the dress-coat for home wear and at dinners in houses where one is a familiar guest. It is occasionally seen at the play, too, but it would be incorrect to wear it when accompanying ladies.

The dinner-jacket.

Etiquette is not now nearly so strict as it used to be in the matter of evening dress in the stalls, private boxes, and dress circle of the theatres. I think this is rather to be deplored, but the wave of democracy that has poured over society of late has left its impress in this as in other matters. Though theatre managers put on the tickets special to the best seats "Even-

On evening dress at theatres.

ing Dress," I have seen half-a-dozen men in the stalls dressed in a variety of unorthodox fashions, and once, in August, I even saw a man in a boating suit come in, straw hat in hand, and, ushered by an unprotesting attendant, take his seat. In the off-season, when all the fashionable people are out of town, this was not, perhaps, very surprising. But he must have been a courageous young man.

A courageous young man.

Mourning for men seems almost a dead-letter nowadays, except in the first two or three weeks after bereavement. A widower's mourning is not worn for more than a couple of months, unless the widower should belong to the numerous class who cling conservatively to old customs, and believe that to doff his weeds would imply some disrespect to his late wife.

Mourning dress.

Disraeli, in his "Endymion," puts the following words in the mouth of Mr. Vigo, the great tailor :—

"Dress does not make a man, but it often makes a successful one. The most precious stone, you know, must be cut and polished. I have known many an heiress lost by her suitor being ill-dressed. You must dress according to your age, your pursuits, your object in life ; you must dress, too, in some cases, according to your set. In youth a little fancy is

"Dress does not make a man."

rather expected, but if political life be your object, it should be avoided—at least after one-and-twenty. I am dressing two brothers now, men of considerable position; one is a mere man of pleasure, the other will probably be a Minister of State. They are as like as two peas, but were I to dress the dandy and the minister the same, it would be bad taste—it would be ridiculous. No man gives me the trouble which Lord Eglantine does; he has not made up his mind whether he will be a great poet or a Prime Minister. 'You must choose, my lord,' I tell him. 'I cannot send you out looking like Lord Byron if you mean to be a Canning or a Pitt.'

"But it often makes a successful one."

"What all men should avoid is the 'shabby genteel.' No man ever gets over it. I will save you from that. You had better be in rags."

COUNTRY LIFE.

DRESS in the country varies considerably in many matters from that worn in town. A boy's first "country suit" after he leaves school is a great event to him. At Eton and Harrow the style of dress might almost be called a uniform, and the first suit of tweeds marks the emancipation from school-life. When in the country he dons these the first thing in the morning, unless he should be on hunting or bicycling thoughts intent, or should incline towards tennis, boating, or the slow delights of angling. After lunch a change has occasionally to be made.

Dress in the country.

The first suit of tweeds.

Should a garden party be in question, he may take his choice between tweed suit and low hat or cutaway coat with silk hat. If he happen to be great on tennis the tweed suit would be naturally his choice, unless it were distinctly understood that the game would form a prominent feature of the afternoon's entertainment. In this case flannels would be worn. Sometimes very ceremonious garden parties

At a garden party.

take place in the country, when Royalty or distinguished persons are expected to be present, when the frock coat and its usual accompaniments would not be out of place.

Invitations to breakfast in the country are by no means unusual. The dress would consist of that **Invitations to breakfast.** ordinarily worn in the mornings, whether tweed suit, knickerbockers, hunting or riding gear, or the black morning-coat or suit. Frequently a silk hat is never seen between Sunday and Sunday. Churchgoers still, to a certain extent, affect it, but in these days of outdoor life, bicycling, and so on, the costume worn by men in church is **Church-going costume.** experiencing the same modifications that characterise it in other departments. The details of shooting suits can always be studied in the illustrated advertisements of the tailors. A man's wardrobe is now almost as varied as a woman's. He has different costumes for walking, riding, driving, visiting, boating, hunting, shooting, golfing, bicycling, tennis, and cricket, dining, smoking, and lounging, football, racing, and yachting, to say nothing of uniform and Court suit, besides the now developing motor-car costume.

IT is necessary for every young man to have a supply of visiting-cards, and for these there is one fixed rule, any departure from which betokens want of knowledge of the customs of well-bred people. The size must be exactly three inches by one and a half. The pasteboard must be pure white and glossy and the lettering must be in italic.

Visiting-cards, size and style.

An idea prevails among young men of a certain class that it is incorrect to put the title "Mr." before their own name on a visiting-card. This is a great mistake. Not to put it is to show oneself lacking in *savoir faire*. The name must always be preceded by "Mr." or "Sir," or other title. The address must occupy the left-hand corner, and the name of one's club or clubs must follow it.

The customary or other title must precede the name.

When a young man has no permanent address, it is well to have only his name printed, filling in the address in pencil before leaving or presenting his card.

In the absence of a permanent address.

The hours for calling are from four to seven in the afternoon, but young men who are not on very intimate terms with the family should carefully abstain from calling after six o'clock, lest they should be the last and solitary caller.

The hours for calling.

When the door is opened, and the question, "Is Mrs. Blank at home?" answered in the affirmative, the visitor is invited to follow the servant. He may take off his overcoat if he wishes, but he must carry his hat and stick in his hand. The right-hand glove must be removed. The gloved hand is never given to a lady, certain exceptional circumstances proving the rule. Arrived in the drawing-room, he holds his hat and glove in the left hand, greets his hostess first, she shaking hands with him, and then he looks round the room and greets any acquaintance he may recognise, going up to them if he knows them well, bowing if his previous knowledge of them has been slight. Having taken his seat, he still holds his hat in his hand, and he must find small talk as best he can, for sitting silent is awkward for him and distressing to his hostess. She, by the way, will probably say, "Would you not like to put down your hat?" indicating some spot where he may lay it. The reason of carrying the hat to the drawing-room

On arrival.

Greeting the hostess.

is a somewhat subtle one. It is based on the supposition that the masculine caller feels himself privileged in being permitted to pay his respects, and feeling himself on sufferance, is ready to leave in a moment, hat in hand, should he not find his presence agreeable and acceptable.

The reason why the hat is carried.

I have a private theory that this custom is cherished and kept up by men from a conviction that their hats are much safer in their own sight in the drawing-room than they would be downstairs in the hall. New umbrellas have been taken instead of old, as we all know, and new hats are quite as tempting, if not more so.

Do not send your card up when making a call. This is reserved for business men. The servant asks your name, and it must be given very distinctly. It will then be announced in a loud, clear voice when the door is opened. Should the hostess show by her manner that she has not recognised the name, its owner must recall himself to her memory by saying, "I am Mr. So-and-so. I had the pleasure of," &c., &c., explaining the circumstances that led to the call.

The card should not be sent up.

The visiting-card must be left on the hall table when the caller goes away, one card for the ladies of the house, and one for the gentleman or

Leaving the card on departure.

gentlemen, whether these latter have
been present or absent during the
call.

Should the lady called on be " Not
at home" the cards are given to the
servant.

When a man has rendered an unknown lady some really important
service, as in the case of a
Rendering an street accident or some other
important
service.   disagreeable circumstance in
which he has been able to
avert from her some unpleasantness
which she would have otherwise in-
curred, the lady will probably ask him
to let her know to whom she is in-
debted for so much kindness. The
proper course to pursue is to disclaim
any special obligation, but if the lady
persists, it is then good manners to
give the name. Should the gentleman
feel very much interested in the lady,
he may say, " I should very much like
to call to-morrow to find out if you are
none the worse for your adventure."
She may then give him her address,
and he would give her his card.

But this would all be very much out
of place if the affair had been some
mere matter of common
A trivial   courtesy, such as picking up
service.   some article dropped by a
lady and restoring it to her. A gentleman in such circumstances raises his
hat and retires as quickly as possible,
lest the lady should imagine that he
could base a claim to her acquaintance

on the performance of so trivial a service.

It is only the " cad " who thus presumes, and the " cad-ess " who allows him to do so.

Visiting-cards are never sent by post. They denote a call in person. The only exception to this rule **P. P. C. Cards.** is in sending out P. P. C. cards. These are always sent by post. The letters denote *pour prendre congé* (" to take leave "), and are used when it is found impossible to call and say goodbye to all one's circle of acquaintance.

A call after a ball or dinner-party must be made within the week, and cards left. In calling to inquire after the welfare of an invalid, or after the family has suffered bereavement, cards are always left. **Sickness and death.** If a man is on intimate terms with a family that has suffered bereavement, he sometimes uses cards with a slight line of black, and should he write a letter of condolence, note-paper and envelopes with the same slight indication of mourning on them. This expresses sympathy and a personal share in the sorrow felt.

In making a call after death has visited any family, the dress of the caller should be attuned to the occasion, and should be of a sombre order, though it need not be precisely mourning.

When a man is a frequent visitor to

any house, he may leave his hat and stick in the hall.

The umbrella is never taken into a drawing-room.

After an invitation. Cards must be left after an invitation, whether the latter be accepted or not.

In case of not wishing to pursue the acquaintance of the person who sent the invitation, it is sufficient to leave the cards without inquiring whether the lady is at home.

If a man should wish, for any reason, to courteously end an acquaintanceship,

Terminating an acquaintanceship with courtesy. he can do it without any of the intolerable "cutting," a method resorted to only by the rough and uncultivated.

He may make a call that, in his own mind, he knows to be a final one, remaining only just the quarter of an

The final call. hour that is the minimum length of such functions, and preserving a certain gravity of demeanour which is as free from "sulks" as it is from other forms of bad temper. After this, he may leave cards once more without asking if the ladies of the family are at home. In this way he can gradually and with perfect courtesy break off the intimacy.

In the street. In the street he raises his hat but does not stop to speak. It is quite possible to ignore the attempt to do so on the opposite side, but should circumstances be such as to make it difficult to do so without positive rudeness, he must stop, putting an end to the conversation at the earliest possible moment.

A call should never extend over half an hour unless the caller be expressly requested to prolong it. A *Duration of call* gentleman never looks at his watch during a call, at a dinner-party, afternoon reception or ball. This is prohibited because the inference would be that *Consulting the watch.* time was dragging with him and that he was anxious to get away. A man may feel such anxiety, but he must hide it if he would be deemed well-bred.

Young men who do not pay their duty call and leave a card after any entertainment, are likely to be omitted from the list of guests invited on some succeeding occasion.

Occasionally it happens that a young man finds himself "dropped" by some family with whom he has *When a man finds himself "dropped."* been on terms of intimacy. He is debarred by the rules of polite society from asking for an explanation, it being a canon of good breeding never to ask questions that are embarrassing to reply to. This has been embodied in a very outspoken and unceremonious phrase "you ask me no questions, I tell you no lies." There is a deep truth in it, nevertheless, and even in family life it is well to observe it.

Sometimes the reason a young man

is dropped in this way is that something to his disadvantage has been discovered. But not unfrequently the true reason is that one of the daughters of the house has shown a preference for his society which the parents think should be checked. Girls of the present day do not always exercise the well-bred self-control that is the rule of good society in such matters. To love unsought is a misfortune for any girl, leading inevitably to much mortification and humiliation, but these may be minimised if she can only practise a dignified reticence about her feelings.

An occasional reason.

But should a young man thus capriciously (as it seems to him) be left out in the cold be on sufficiently good terms with a son of the house, it would be quite in rule for him to put out a feeler or two on the subject : " I say, old fellow, I wonder if I have been so unfortunate as to offend your people in any way ? " He will soon discover, from the aspect of his interlocutor, whether he is likely to gain any information on the matter.

Putting out a feeler.

CALLS OF INQUIRY.

In calling on friends who have suffered bereavement, after having received their card of thanks for kind inquiries, it is, of course, requisite that the dress should

be of the quietest description. A red
tie, for instance, would be horribly out
of place. Only in case of
very intimate friendships is
the call prolonged beyond
ten minutes or a quarter
of an hour. The caller takes his
tone from that of the family. It is
in the worst taste to refer to the
loss sustained unless the initiative is
taken by one of those
bereaved. This is very
seldom done, and the
conversation is usually con-
ducted on lines calculated to avert any
disturbing remark. No one likes to
break down or lose self-command
except in seclusion; and, in fact, it
is only necessary to look into one's
own consciousness in order to discover what is the best course to
follow in such cases.

Calling on friends bereaved.

Avoiding reference to the loss.

Should a young man be invited to
attend the funeral, he must wear
mourning, black gloves, and
black hatband. Punctuality,
important at all times, is
particularly essential at this dreary
ceremonial. The family usually provides carriages, but in the case of
friends who possess equipages, they
always take their own. It is the
custom to assemble at the house, or
to go by fixed train should
the family reside in the
country. It is better not
to accept any invitations to return to

Attending the funeral.

Invitations to return.

the house afterwards; for, as a rule, these are only given as a matter of form.

We often see in newspapers after the announcement of a death, a request that no flowers may be sent. Failure to comply with this would argue a want of perception, but when no such intimation is made a friend may send flowers, the only essential being that they should consist as a rule of pure white flowers or orchids, pansies, or violets. Occasionally an exception is made to these in the case of favourite flowers of the lost friend. An exquisite garland of pale tea-roses appeared among the scores of wreaths seen at the funeral of one of our greatest poets.

Gifts of flowers:

MANNER.

It would not be easy to over-estimate the importance of a good manner from a social point of view. It ranks far above much more important qualities. The "rough diamonds" who conceal their traditional good heart under a surly exterior are seldom happy people, notwithstanding their genuine thoroughness and real goodness. In family life and in society a gentle manner "covers a multitude of sins." The world and the home reflect back to us the face we present to them. If we cultivate a bright and cordial manner we shall be heartily received by others, though the real nature of us lies beneath as cold and hard as salt fresh from a mine. In the home the coldness and hardness are soon found out, but they are partially condoned for the sake of the superficial courtesy and kindness. In society the quality of the heart matters little, so long as the surface is, at the same time, genial and polished. Life is chiefly made up of small things, and if we learn to take an interest in

The importance of a good manner.

The qualities valued by society.

"Life is a large bundle of little things."

the trifling incidents of our friends' lives, in the everyday occurrences in the existence of our acquaintances, we supply the sympathetic element that tells so largely in our favour. And very often the simulation of this interest induces the reality, and our own life is brightened by participating in the pleasures and the happiness of others, and deepened by sharing in their disappointments, and by doing so helping them to overcome them. With a cold, forbidding manner it is impossible to convey any such impression. But this often comes from shyness, not only in the young, but all through life. The youthful form of shyness is self-consciousness and self-distrust. That which lasts through life is the fear of self-revelation. Even the frankest natures have often this quality of reticence, which forbids them to reveal the inner depths of their thoughts, and makes them hate to be divined.

Simulation may induce reality.

Shyness.

And reticence.

Rochefoucauld says we all hate to be divined, though we like to divine others ; but many of us know well what a delightful thing it is to be read like an open book by those whose thoughts reflect our own, and with whom we discover ourselves to be in mental kinship.

The ideal life is that which has few friends but many acquaintances. The

friends are close and firm ones, "grappled to our hearts with hooks of steel,"
and the circle of acquaintances offers opportunities for adding to their number. But without an agreeable manner it is difficult to secure these inner and outer spheres of social companionship. Were I asked to give a recipe for the formation of a good manner I should recommend an equal mixture of self-confidence and humility as the first essential, then a considerable desire to please, tempered by the self-respect which preserves from officiousness and that annoying air of "ingratiating" themselves that some men assume in society. There must be perfect self-possession, though in the very young this is scarcely expected, a little becoming shyness sitting very well upon them. "I like a shy man. He's getting so scarce," said a very pretty woman at a ball not long since. "Find one, quick, and introduce him." Her laughing emissaries went off to search for the desired article, and after a while returned with the report that the only shy man in the room was engaged for every dance!

When self-possession has been acquired it is well to add on to it the saving grace of gentleness. This quality is much misunderstood by men. In women they adore it; in

The ideal life—few friends, many acquaintances.

A recipe for the formation of a good manner.

Add gentleness to self-possession.

themselves and each other they under-
value it. But women love gentleness
in men. It is a most telling piece of
the necessary equipment for society.
A gentle manner, a gentle voice, and
the absence of all self-assertion that
is at the root of the matter, have won
more love than good looks.

Carlyle called the members of upper-
class society "amiable stoics," in reference to the equable serenity
of countenance and calm
self-possession of manner
with which they accept those occasionally trying conditions of social life
which necessitate self-denial in matters
great and small. This placidity is the
result of long training. Not just at
first does a young man bow to the
decree of his hostess which separates
him from the girl he admires and tells
him off to take some uninteresting
dowager to the supper-room. But
should he evince any sign of discon-
tent with the arrangement he is at
once convicted of ill-breeding. The
man of "perfect manners"
is he who is calmly cour-
teous in all circumstances,
as attentive outwardly to
the plain and the elderly as he is to
the young and pretty. It is difficult to
renounce the delightful *tête-à-tête* with
a charming girl when asked by his
hostess to dance with some poor wallflower who has been neglected for
half-a-dozen dances. But it has to

"Amiable stoics."

The man of "perfect manners."

134

be borne, and eventually it brings its own reward. The "duty" dance is a hard thing, and good man- *Self-denial not unrewarded.* ners involve a considerable amount of self-denial; but repetition soon makes it comparatively easy, and invitations of an agreeable kind pour in on the young man who shows himself willing to practise those peculiar forms of self-lessness, opportunities for which so frequently arise in society.

It is probably in imitation of this surface equanimity that the wooden stare has been adopted so *The wooden stare.* universally by our golden youth. This is useful for wearing at one's club or in the stall of a theatre, and it at once stamps the proprietor of the stare as being "in it." The fashion is not confined to England. It reigns in New York, and even in far Australia there is a select coterie of golden or gilded youth who are beginning to learn how to abstract every atom of expression from the countenance, and to look on vacancy or seem to do so. As yet, there is no considerable expertness achieved in the matter in Antipodean circles, but in New York a very fair impression of imbecility is conveyed in the look of the ultra-fashionable young man. There are various other important matters on which a transatlantic authority has been instructing the youth of his generation. The one involving the most serious responsibility is connected with carrying a cane or stick, as it is better form to call it. It must be left at home when going to business, to church, or to make calls. The idea of the latter prohibition is that, if a call is made on a lady cane in hand, the inference would be that the caller is on sufficiently intimate terms to look in on her casually at any time. There is certainly subtlety in this view. It is well that the novice should be made aware that the lowest depth of vulgarity is touched by carrying an umbrella in a case. It is also an important item of information that the gloves and cane must be carried in the same hand. To do otherwise is seriously to err in social forms. Our instructor declares that to attend oratorios and philharmonic concerts is thoroughly bad form, indicating a tendency to be pedantic. It is much better to go to a horse show. It is by no means considered correct to shake hands. The proper way is to take hold of the fingers of one's acquaintance at the second joints, and bestow upon them one or two decisive little jerks, as though testing their strength. "No, I thank you," is a form of words no longer heard in good society, having some time since been replaced by "No, thanks." No man with any claim to social position would consent to pronounce the "g" at the end of the

Transatlantic etiquette.

present participle of verbs. "Comin' and goin'" are the correct forms just now. "Don't you know" is ridiculously correct. Men of perception do not care to be more accurate than others of their set. "Don't-chi-know" is more customary, and the pronunciation marks the man as riding on the topmost crest of the social wave. There must be a staccato sound about the phrase, which alternates pleasantly with the languid drawl. The latter is still in favour, and accompanies admirably the studied lack of animation in the expression and general wooden look of the face.

To revert for a moment to the cane, or walking-stick. There is much to be deduced from the manner in which it

The stick. is carried. The correct style is to hold it at an angle of forty-five degrees, with the ferule uppermost and forward. This is the sort of thing that no man could possibly discover for himself. The natural man would incline to carry his stick in such fashion as would tend to direct its point to the ground. This unsophisticated mode would at once reveal him as uninitiated in the minor morals of good

The hair. manners. The latest mode of arranging the male hair, as practised in New York, and possibly nearer home as well, is worth noting. First it is made thoroughly wet, then brushed and parted, after which the head is swathed with linen bands.

which are kept on until the hair is thoroughly dry. This method produces the plastered appearance which is now recognised as good form. Though cordiality of manner is rapidly becoming obsolete, and is utterly condemned by all who have studied the subject,

Amiability. yet it is a recognised fact that amiability has now superseded sarcasm, and the up-to-date young man practises a careless superficial benevolence of pronouncing every woman charming and every man a good fellow. The scathing, satiric wit of the last century was as the nadir to this zenith of appreciative recognition of the best that is in every human being.

It is pleasant to be able to add to all this minute detail about little superficialities that the young man of to-day is a vast improvement on his predecessors in very many ways. Swearing is out of fashion. Getting intoxicated is decidedly "low," and those who disgrace themselves in this way are soon cut by their acquaint-

The rowdy-ism of twenty years ago. ance. Some twenty years since things were very different. To get tipsy was regarded as a proof of manliness. To wrench off door-knockers and play similar senseless pranks was considered a form of wit, and the heroes of such performances were looked on with admiring eyes by their companions.

In many ways a higher standard now

reigns. The pictures of ballet dancers
that used once to adorn a
young man's rooms have
given place to others of a
higher class. Dissolute and
unprincipled men get the cold shoulder
from others of their set, and vice, thank
Heaven, is thoroughly out of fashion.
There is still plenty of folly. It is
inseparable from youth. But in matters
of more moment there has been im-
mense improvement going steadily on
for many years.

A higher moral stand- ard now reigns.

There are young men who mistake
arrogance of manners for self-possession, and who conduct
themselves, when in society
with lifted chin and a
haughty air that may accord very well
with their own estimate of themselves,
but seem rather out of place to on-
lookers. Such a man invites com-
parisons between his social deserts and
his implied conviction of superiority.
He may take in a few inexperienced
girls and young fellows of adolescent
inability of judgment, but even these
triumphs are short-lived, and he is set
down as a " pompous ass," to use the
young man's phrase for describing him.

Arrogance of manners.

It is good manners to articulate
distinctly, and bad manners to neglect
to do so. A man need not
exactly take lessons in elo-
cution (though they would
not be amiss), but he can teach himself to pronounce clearly and use the

Distinct articulation.

tone of voice that is best suited to the various occasions when he converses. A breathy voice is extremely disagreeable. The syllables come out enveloped in a sort of windy roar. This is owing to a wrong way of breathing, and it can easily be cured, with advantage to the health as well as the personality. A very confidential tone is always used by some men when they speak to women. If they merely "hope your gown did not get muddy" they look into one's eyes and murmur like any sucking dove. But if their articulation is indistinct they are quite a nuisance. One has to ask them to repeat themselves, and the nonsense they talk shows up very badly in an *encore*. But when they enunciate clearly their devoted murmurings sometimes "take" very well. It is not until a woman has seen three or four others besides herself approached in the same afternoon or evening with similar devout and prayer-like whispering that she begins to value this particularity at its true worth.

Tones of voice.

The confidential tone.

With reference to the word "fellow" a subtle distinction or two must be drawn. In lowly circles a young man is called "a fellow"; young men "fellows." So it is in good society, but with a distinct difference. It is not very easy to make this difference clear. Young men of good position refer very

The word "fellow."

commonly to others of their acquaintance as "the fellows," but they would not use the word to describe young men generally. Women, young and old, of the lower classes speak of young men generally as "fellows," but gentlewomen never do so. A lady never uses the expression "A girl and a fellow." At the same time she may frequently speak of "young fellows." I am aware that there is a want of clearness in all this, but it is a matter among many others that can only be acquired by being accustomed to the usages of good society.

The Autocrat of the Breakfast-table said in one of his books that if he heard a woman pronounce the word "How," he learned more about her in an instant than a third person could tell him in an hour. If she called it "haow," she revealed herself as belonging to the uncultured classes. In the same way, if a girl were to say "I met a fellow yesterday," she would unconsciously make a similar self-revelation. A young man would make an equal mistake if he were to speak of "my sister's fellow." But he would be correct enough if he were to say "the fellow my sister's engaged to."

The "Autocrat's" test-word.

"Tweedle-dum and tweedledee."

These little *nuances* of expression remind one of the old rhyme—

"Strange that such difference should be
'Twixt tweedledum and tweedledee."

Though small talk is as indispensable in social life as pennies and half-pennies in the transactions of everyday existence, we must also have conversational gold and silver at our command if we wish to be successful. When the preliminaries of acquaintanceship are over there is no necessity to keep up the commonplaces of small talk. To do so is rather insulting to women. To be "talked down to" is always aggravating, especially when one feels a conviction that the person who is thus affably stooping for one's benefit belongs in reality to a lower intellectual plane than one's own. At the same time, many young men "with nothing in them" are socially successful, being possessed of those superficial qualities and that outward polish which are, for the purposes of everyday intercourse, more useful than abysmal personal depths. Was it Goethe or Schiller who said that for domestic utility a farthing candle is more useful than all the stars of heaven?

A light playfulness of fancy, combined with the gentleness that carefully avoids wounding even the smallest, is a high recommendation in society; but to be for ever laughing is wearisome in the extreme to the spectators.

I make no apology for quoting here

Small talk alone will not suffice.

"Talking down" really an insult.

Yet polish alone often succeeds.

the following passages from "Mr.
Brown's Letters to a Young
Man About Town" from a
Punch of 1849. "Mr. Brown"
was Thackeray, I believe.
He says :—

*"Mr.
Brown's"
advice.*

"I beseech and implore you to
make a point of being intimate with
one or two families where you can
see kind and well-bred English ladies.
I have seen women of all nations in
the world, but I never saw the equals
of English women (meaning, of course,
to include our cousins the MacWhirters
of Glasgow and the O'Tooles of Cork) ;
and I pray sincerely, my boy, that
you may always have a woman for a
friend."

*   *   *   *

"It is better for you to pass an evening once or twice a week in a lady's
drawing-room, even though the conversation is rather slow and you know
the girl's songs by heart, than in a club,
tavern, or smoking-room, or pit of a
theatre."

*   *   *   *

"Remember, if a house is pleasant,
and you like to remain in it, that to be
well with the women of the house is the
great, the vital point. If it is a good
house, don't turn up your nose because
you are only asked to come in the evening, while others are invited to dine.
Recollect the debts of dinners which

an hospitable family has to pay ; who are you that you should always be expecting to nestle under the mahogany ? Agreeable acquaintances are made just as well in the drawing-room as in the dining-room. Go to tea brisk and good-humoured. Be determined to be pleased. Talk to a dowager. Take a hand at whist. If you are musical, and know a song, sing it like a man. Never sulk about dancing, but off with you. You will find your acquaintance enlarge. Mothers, pleased with your good humour, will probably ask you to Pocklington Square, to a little party. You will get on—you will form yourself a circle. You may marry a rich girl, or, at any rate, get the chance of seeing a number of the kind and the pretty."

*   *   *   *

" The dressing, the clean gloves, and cab-hire, are nuisances, I grant you. The idea of the party itself is a bore, but you must go. When you are at the party, it is not so stupid ; there is always something pleasant for the eye and attention of an observant man."

IN CHURCH.

I KNOW a young man who makes it a practice to arrive late in church every Sunday. I often wish On arriving late at church. that he did not go to my church, for he makes me cordially despise him, thus disturbing the calm and quiet of the proper frame of mind for Sundays. I conclude that he likes to be looked at, though why he should do so is not apparent. It is, in fact, not only rude, but irreverent, to be late in church for the beginning of the service. If one should be accidentally late, it is good manners to wait till the congregation rises from the kneeling posture before making one's way to a seat. It is almost an awful thing to interrupt a prayer. But I have seen people do it with no more scruple than if they were passing in a crowded street.

Eighteen inches are the measurement of space allowed to each sitter in the churches. In some On the space one may occupy. it may be more; in others it may be less. But I have reason to believe that this is the average. Now, if any man of extra size should find himself in a pew with other persons, he must, in

common courtesy, keep himself as
well within the limits of eighteen
inches as the width of his shoulders
will allow. But I have occasionally
seen quite slim young men sprawl far
beyond the frontier lines. Lounging

Lounging. is a habit of the day, and
there are men who get themselves into marvellously corkscrew
attitudes, in church as elsewhere.
Fidgety men are more so in church
than anywhere else. They

Fidgety men. seem to find it impossible to
keep still. Sometimes they
even produce a cough wherewith to
amuse themselves, though they are
not troubled with it at any other time.
The charm of a reposeful manner is
denied to them. Reverence for the
sacred place conduces to a quiet
manner ; but this is not always felt
by those who attend public worship.

The conventional idea of church attendance. The conventional idea seems
to be that such assemblies
are merely phases of social
life ; that it is respectable to
be seen there ; and that the service
and the sermon are things to be
worried through in deference to a
prevalent idea that they form part
of an institution that is generally
regarded as excellent. The small

The true light to regard the services in. minority are those who regard church services in their
true light as lifting the
thoughts above earthly
things, and yet by no means unfitting

them for earth. Where, for instance, could a better law of good manners be found than in the Book of Books? A glance at the end of the fourth chapter of Ephesians will show a code of conduct that, if followed, would make a man a perfect member of society.

CORRESPONDENCE.

It is impolite to leave letters un-
answered for several days, especially if
Replying to
letters.
the writers are ladies, or, if
men, superior in age or
station. Notes of invitation
should be replied to within twenty-four
hours. Plain white cream-laid note-
paper and envelopes should be used,
Writing
materials.
the latter either square or
wallet-shaped, but never of
the oblong, narrow shape
peculiar to business correspondence.
The address on the notepaper should
be embossed or printed in simple
characters, over-ornament being in the
worst taste. If the writer is entitled
to use a crest, it should be produced as
simply as possible, with or without the
family motto, and free from the glow
of varied colour in which some men
and women delight. There are letters
whose devices in scarlet and gold are
strangely in contrast with the meagre
and disappointing character of their
contents. They make one think of
fried sprats served up on a gold entrée
dish.

The writing should be clear, neat

and legible, the ink black. In beginning a letter with " Sir " or " Madam,"
the omission of the name is remedied
by inscribing it in the left-
The addressee's name. hand corner at the bottom
of the note. In commercial
correspondence it seems to
be the rule to put the name of the
addressee just above " Dear Sir " or
" Madam."

Should it be advisable to enclose in
any letter an envelope for a reply,
ready addressed, it is not
Enclosing reply envelopes. good form to put " Esq."
after one's own name in
addressing it.

Married women and widows are not
addressed by their own Christian
names, but by those of their
Addressing married women. husbands. For instance, no
one versed in social forms
would write " Mrs. Mary
Smith," but " Mrs. John Smith."
Widows of titled men have their
Christian name put before their surname, thus, " Laura Lady Ledding,"
Maria Marchioness of Adesbury,"
Georgina Viscountess Medway," " Mary
Duchess of Blankton." The unmarried
daughters of dukes, marquises, and
earls have their Christian name invariably inserted between their courtesy
title and surname, as : " Lady Mary
Baker." When married they retain
this form, only substituting the husband's surname for their own, as
" Lady Mary Garth." But if their

husband should be a peer, they merge their courtesy title in his.

The third person in correspondence is falling considerably into disuse, and "presenting compliments" is almost obsolete. Invitations of a formal kind, and their replies, are couched in the third person, but for pur-

Use of the third person. poses of correspondence with strangers it is almost always better to use the first person. The exception is in replying to a letter written in the third person, when it is in better taste to reply in the same way. The third person is also used in writing to tradespeople : "Mr. Edlicott will feel obliged if Mr. Jones will kindly call on Thursday morning with reference to some repairs." In this case the reply would be written in the first person.

Letters of introduction, says La Fontaine, "are drafts that must be cashed at sight." They are sometimes difficult to write, especially if they have been asked for, not volun-

Letters of introduction. teered. They are always left unsealed, but should there be circumstances about the person introduced which the other party should know, it is well to communicate them in a private letter, which should be despatched so as to arrive before the letter of introduction is presented. Any one receiving a letter of introduction would immediately take steps to show some attention to the individual introduced. The usual thing is to ask him to dinner, if he is a social equal; to offer his services, if he should be a superior; and to ascertain in what way one can be useful to him, if he is an inferior. A personal call must precede all invitations. This is a fixed and rigid rule, the exception being in the case of persons presenting their own letters of introduction, as is usually done. But should the person to whom they are addressed be out, the formal call must follow.

A call must precede invitations.

All ladies, from the Queen downwards, are addressed in beginning a letter as "Madam"; all gentlemen, from the highest to the lowest, as "Sir." Tradesmen, however, begin "Your Royal Highness," "Your Grace," or "Your Ladyship," in writing to their titled employers. They also address their letters quite differently, as will be seen from the following instructions :—

Styles of address at the beginning of a letter.

ADDRESSES OF LETTERS.

Her Majesty the Queen.

To His Royal Highness the Prince of Wales.

To Her Royal Highness the Princess of Wales.

This same form is used in addressing communications to all other members of the Royal Family, adding the title where the word "Prince" or "Princess" would be incorrect, as :—

To His Royal Highness the Duke of York.

To Her Royal Highness the Duchess of York.

Below the rank of royalty there is the distinction between letters addressed by persons on an equality with those to whom they write, and by inferiors. I shall call them formal and informal, and range them in separate lines.

Address for the envelope —formal and informal.

Informal.	Formal.
The Duke of ——	To His Grace the Duke of ——
The Duchess of ——	To Her Grace the Duchess of ——
The Marquis of ——	To the Most Honourable the Marquis of ——
The Marchioness of —	To the Most Honourable the Marchioness of ——
The Earl of ——	To the Right Honourable the Earl of ——
The Countess of ——	To the Right Honourable the Countess of ——
The Viscount ——	The Right Honourable the Viscount ——
The Viscountess ——	The Right Honourable the Viscountess——
Lord ——	The Right Honourable Lord — or Baron —-
Lady ——	The Right Honourable Lady —— or Baroness ——

Members of the Privy Council are

also addressed as "Right Honourable," in the same way as Peers.

In this case the names of commoners are not followed by the abbreviation "Esq.," as :—

The Right Honourable James Balfour, M.P.

Ambassadors and their wives are addressed as "His Excellency," "Her Excellency," the personal and official titles following the word, as :—

To His Excellency the Earl of ——, Ambassador Extraordinary and Pleni-potentiary to France.

To Her Excellency the Countess of ——.

Other official personages are addressed in the following way :—

To His Excellency Lord Blank, Lord Lieutenant of Ireland.

To His Grace the Archbishop of ——.

The Right Reverend the Bishop of ——

The Very Reverend the Dean of ——.

Academical distinctions are indicated by the initials placed after the name—LL.D. for Doctor of Laws and Learning, D.D. for Doctor of Divinity and so on.

So much for the envelopes. The proper way to begin letters is as follows. As I have mentioned, the Queen is addressed as " Madam " in the inside of a letter. A gentleman writing to the Queen would sign himself, " I have the honour to submit myself, with profound respect, Your Majesty's most devoted subject and servant." Above the word "Madam" should be written "Her Majesty the Queen." Lord Beaconsfield struck out a line of his own and in writing to the Queen began, "Mr. Disraeli," continuing in the third person and addressing Her Majesty in the second. The Prince of Wales is addressed as "Sir," above this word being written "To His Royal Highness the Prince of Wales." Persons on intimate terms sometimes begin "Sir" or "Dear Prince," others "My dear Prince." The Princess of Wales is occasionally addressed by friends as "My dear Princess." The two orthodox endings to such letters are respectively "Your Royal Highness's dutiful and obedient servant," or (a humbler style) "Your Royal Highness's dutiful and most obedient servant." To all other Royal Princes and Princesses the ending would be "Most Humble and Obedient Servant." Dukes other than royal are addressed inside letters by intimates as "Dear Duke," by others "My Lord Duke, may it please your Grace." In writing to a Duchess her title is placed above the "Madam." In formal letters Marquises would be addressed as "My Lord Marquis."

To the Queen.

To the Prince and Princess of Wales.

To a Duke and Duchess.

A very common form of mistake is that of omitting the christian name from the courtesy titles of the sons and daughters of dukes, marquises, and earls. The sons have the title " Lord " prefixed to the christian and surname : for instance, " Lord Alfred Osborne," " Lord Henry Somerset." It is extremely incorrect to call either of these " Lord Osborne " or " Lord Somerset." The daughters of dukes, marquises and earls have the title " Lady " before their christian and surname; " Lady Emily Heneage," for instance, must not be addressed as " Lady Heneage." Should she marry a commoner only the surname is altered, the " Lady Emily " remains. This may all appear a little involved to those unaccustomed to titles, but neglect of these forms indicates very clearly a lack of *savoir faire*. It is a source of great annoyance to the owners of courtesy titles to have the christian name omitted. Anybody, even a knight's wife, may be a " Lady Smith " or " Jones " ; the insertion of the christian name before the " Smith " or " Jones " means that the possessor is the daughter of a duke, marquis, or earl.

In beginning a letter to any of the above a stranger would say " Dear Lady Mary Smith," but the usual form would be " Dear Lady Mary." Inferiors would begin by writing the lady's title over the word " Madam," or

On omitting christian names from courtesy titles.

Beginning a letter to the above.

merely beginning "Madam" and writing the title at the end of the letter.

In writing to an ambassador or his wife the title is placed above the word "Sir" or "Madam." Inferiors would write "May it please your Excellency," and would conclude with "I have the honour to be Your Excellency's most humble, obedient servant."

To an ambassador, with conclusion.

In writing to an archbishop a correspondent would begin "Your Grace," ending, "I remain Your Grace's most obedient servant."

An archbishop.

To a bishop the form would be, "My Lord," or "Right Reverend Sir," or "May it please Your Lordship," the last being, of course, the humblest form of address. The conclusion would be, "I remain, My Lord," (or "Right Reverend Sir") "Your most obedient servant."

A bishop.

The beginning of a letter to a dean would be, "Reverend Sir" or "Mr. Dean," the title of all these dignitaries being, in formal letters, indited above the beginning. Those having some acquaintance would begin, "Dear Mr. Dean." Strangers would end the letter, "I have the honour to be Your most obedient servant."

A dean.

Doctors of divinity are addressed as "Reverend Sir," as well as archdeacons and all other clergy.

Doctors of Divinity.

Intimates would begin letters to the above with : " Dear Archbishop," " Dear Bishop," " Dear Dean," or " Dear Doctor."

With the sole exception of lieutenants in the army, all officers have their military rank prefixed **Officers in the army,** to their name. Lieutenants are addressed as " Esq." In the navy admirals of the flag—white, blue, or red—are addressed **And navy.** as " The Honourable," this being prefixed to the name. Otherwise a letter would begin " Sir," and end, " I remain, Sir, Your obedient servant." Commodores, captains, and lieutenants in the navy are all addressed in the same way.

PERSONAL SPEECH WITH
ROYALTY AND RANK.

It is sometimes difficult to know how to address personally people of high rank. The Queen is ad-

Addressing the Queen in person. dressed as " Ma'am " by those immediately sur-

rounding her person and by princesses, duchesses, and others who are on terms that may be de-scribed as those of acquaintanceship with her Majesty. All others would speak to her as "Your Majesty."

The Princess of Wales and all other princesses are in the same

The Princess of Wales. way addressed as " Ma'am," or "Your Royal Highness,"

according to the position of the person speaking to them.

The Prince of Wales, with all other royal dukes and princes, is addressed as "Sir," or "Your Royal

The Prince of Wales and royal dukes. Highness"; the Duke of Teck as "Your Highness,"

as well as many foreign princes. Equals would address all these as " Prince."

The following list will show the correct modes of addressing

Formal and informal modes of addressing nobility in person. the nobility informally and formally, in conversation, the first being the custom among acquaintances, the

latter by all others :—

PERSONAL SPEECH.

Rank.		Informal.	Formal.
Duke		Duke.	Your Grace.
Duchess.	...	Duchess.	Your Grace.
Marquis... ...		Lord A.	My Lord,
			or
			Your Lordship.
Marchioness...		Lady A.	My Lady,
			or
			Your Ladyship.
Earl		Lord B.	My Lord,
			or
			Your Lordship.
Countess	...	Lady B.	My Lady,
			or
			Your Ladyship.
Viscount	...	Lord C.	My Lord,
			or
			Your Lordship.
Viscountess ...		Lady C.	My Lady,
			or
			Your Ladyship.
Baron		Lord D.	My Lord,
			or
			Your Lordship.
Baroness	...	Lady D.	My Lady,
			or
			Your Ladyship

It is one of the rules of etiquette that, in speaking with royal persons, the inferior leaves it to them to originate subjects of conversation, and never introduces any topic of his own.

Letters of condolence are among the most difficult forms of composition. They are almost equally trying to read and to write. The best rule to be given for these is to make them as brief as possible. If "brevity is the soul of wit," it is also, in such cases, the very heart of sympathy. A very usual fault

committed is to begin by dilating upon
the shock or grief felt by the writer.
The absurdity of this becomes apparent
when one compares mentally the shock
or grief as felt by the recipient. Two
lines conveying the expression of
sympathy are better than pages of
even the most eloquent composition.
Mourners require all their fortitude at
times of loss, and anything likely to
impair their self-command is the
reverse of a kindness.

On hearing or reading of the death
of an acquaintance or friend, an expression of sympathy should at once
be sent off. It used to be the custom
to wait for the memoriam
Memoriam cards. cards sent out by the family,
but this, if it was ever the
custom in the best society, has now
long ceased to be so. Memoriam cards
are only used in humble circles. At
the same time, one needs to be very
careful as to the accuracy of one's
information before sending off a letter
of condolence. Similarity of name is
apt to lead to awkward mistakes. In
this connection it may be as well to
remark that about a week after the
funeral it is customary to
The inquiry call. call and leave cards of
inquiry. When these are
responded to by cards of thanks for
inquiries, it is a sign that the family is
willing to receive callers.

INDEX